Twenty–Two
GAMES OF FAME

A CHRONICLE OF THE 2017 CLEVELAND INDIANS WIN STREAK

TO Greg

GO TRIBE !

Nicholas Brigeman

NICHOLAS BRIGEMAN

PAGE PUBLISHING, INC.
New York, NY

First originally published by Page Publishing, Inc. 2019

Cover Design Andrew Micale

ISBN 978-1-64462-010-6 (Paperback)
ISBN 978-1-64462-011-3 (Digital)

Printed in the United States of America

In Major League Baseball, there is debate as to which franchise holds the record for the longest winning streak. Many baseball analysts and fans say that the streak is held by the 1916 New York Giants who won twenty-six without a loss. Whenever this topic is discussed, fans seem to overlook what happened on September 18, 1916, between the New York Giants and the Pittsburgh Pirates. The Giants were playing for their twelfth straight win when the game was interrupted by heavy rainfall in the eighth inning with the game in a 1–1 tie. By the time the rain had stopped, it was too dark to play, and the game between New York and Pittsburgh was restarted the next day from the beginning. The Giants won the game and proceeded to win the next fourteen games in a row.

Major League Baseball did not have lights for night games until 1935, and the September 18, 1916 game is marked in the record books and is widely recognized as a tie. In 1935, when teams could play ball under the lights, the Chicago Cubs won twenty-one consecutive ball games with no games postponed due to weather or darkness. Fans stated that during the Cleveland Indians' incredible win streak before the team reached twenty-two straight wins, the longest winning streak should belong to the Chicago Cubs and that the New York Giants' streak should be entitled as the longest "unbeaten" streak.

The pages that follow are an in-depth chronicle of every game of the historic 2017 Cleveland Indians' win streak. The author and Indians fans around the country were witnesses to one of the greatest team achievements in sports history, and this book details each game in real time so that fans and sports history buffs alike will be able to look back with great detail into the streak and the incredible team and individual plays that made it possible.

Introduction

On Thursday, August 24, 2017, the Boston Red Sox faced the Cleveland Indians at Progressive Field in Downtown Cleveland. The Red Sox and the Indians were finishing their four-game series with Boston leading the series two games to one, with tonight's first pitch scheduled for 7:10 p.m. The night before, the Indians lost game 3 to Boston by a score of 6–1; the losing pitcher was the Tribe's ace Corey Kluber. Wednesday night's loss gave Kluber a record of 12–4 with a 2.65 ERA, one of the best in the American League. Kluber is once again having a tremendous season and is a top candidate to win his second American League Cy Young Award in four years. In this fourth and final game of the series, the Tribe had their way with the Red Sox ace and Cy Young candidate Chris Sale, scoring seven runs in three innings. In the bottom of the third inning, the Indians' designated hitter, Yandy Díaz, is batting with Cleveland's Brandon Guyer on first and Edwin Encarnacion on second. Both Guyer and Encarnacion are walked by Chris Sale, and Yandy Díaz is batting with only one out in a 4–1 ball game with the Indians on top. Díaz smokes Sale's 1–2 pitch on a line drive into right field over the head of Mookie Betts and off the wall! Encarnacion scores on Díaz RBI double, and Guyer holds at third as Cleveland takes a 5–1 lead.

The Tribe continues to build on their four-run lead when third baseman Giovanny Urshela hits a 2-out, 2-run single to center. "Now the 0–1 pitch swung on banged back up the middle into center. That's a base hit! Guyer scores, Díaz scores, Giovanny Urshela with a 3-RBI night. How about the bottom third tonight!" (Tom Hamilton). The Red Sox starter, Chris Sale, would not return to pitch in the fourth inning, making this the second time in August in which the Indians had scored seven runs while facing Chris Sale. In the bottom of the sixth inning, the Indians' right fielder, Jay Bruce, is batting with Cleveland leading Boston, 8–4, and the bases empty with one out. Bruce is facing Red Sox reliever, Brandon Workman, with a 1–1 count; he is one for three with a groundout in the bottom of the fourth inning. Workman's pitch to Bruce is swung on, and he hits a ball to dead centerfield. It's got a chance…gone! It is a home run ball that barely cleared the nineteen-foot wall in center field, home run number 33 for Jay Bruce!

The Tribe takes a 9–4 lead, and Bruce hits his first home run at Progressive Field since joining the Indians. In the bottom of the seventh inning, Yandy Díaz is at bat with two men on base, with two out, and he is looking to stay perfect on the day. The first pitch by Fernando Abad is offered to Díaz, and he swings and hits his second RBI double of the game into right field. José Ramírez scores from second base to give the Indians a 13–4 lead, and Yandy Díaz goes 4–4 on the game with two RBI doubles, a single and a triple. In the top of the ninth inning, the Red Sox are down to their final out, trailing Cleveland by seven runs. The Indians' reliever, Dan Otero, is facing Andrew Benintendi, who is 1–4 with a strikeout by Bryan Shaw in the seventh. "He fires a swing and a sky ball shallow left. Guyer coming in, he's under it. Ball game! So the Indians split this four-game series with the Red Sox. They rout Chris Sale and the Boston Red Sox tonight," Tom Hamilton says.

Starter Chris Sale takes his sixth loss, giving him a record of 14–6. Tonight's win gives the Indians a record of 70–56 and a five-and-a-half game lead over the second place, Minnesota Twins. Tonight's win by the Indians may seem like just one game of home-cooking for the Tribe, but this win over Boston was the beginning of something truly remarkable. A streak for the ages has just been born. It is a winning streak that would surpass the streak of the 1935 Chicago Cubs and become the longest winning streak in Major League Baseball history! During the win streak, the Cleveland Indians put up some of the most improbable numbers this game has ever seen. The Indians' pitching and hitting was by far superior to the opposition, and very few of the games were even close. The entire pitching staff had a team earned run average (ERA) of 1.78 and a strikeout to walk ratio of 200–37. The Indians' hitters clobbered more home runs than total runs allowed, 41–37. Thirty-six different players played during the win streak, and every game seemingly presented a different star.

Chapter 1

---❯❯❯ ❮❮❮---

MLB Players Weekend, Games 2–4

On August 25, 2017, Major League Baseball debuted a weekend series unlike any other ever staged by the Major Leagues. It is a series that was conceived for the players' enjoyment, giving each of them the opportunity to show off their unique personalities to their teammates and, of course, all the fans. All thirty teams have voted on new colorful caps and jerseys to wear, but the newest and most stunning addition to the uniforms are the nicknames each player has chosen to wear in place of their last name. Every player on the Indians has a story behind the nickname they have chosen. Some players used nicknames they had as a child, others were given a nickname by a teammate or manager when they came into the league.

The Kansas City Royals have flown into town to play a three-game divisional series against the Cleveland Indians for this first ever Players Weekend. In the Indians' clubhouse before game 1, the Indians' left-handed reliever, Andrew "Miller Time" Miller, brought in fifty coolers of Miller Lite to share with his teammates, while shortstop Francisco Lindor commented on the new uniforms, "I just saw Tomlin's (nickname), 'Scrubs' they call him that, but I didn't think he was going to put it. I think that's cool." Although some fans may not understand the reason behind some of the nicknames chosen by the players, it's all in good fun! Many of the Indians players say the new uniforms made them feel like they we're playing in a little league series again. Players across the league have been given new equipment to use like socks, bats, wristbands, and cleats.

During Players Weekend, the Indians would have all the fun and all the runs. The team's hitting and pitching is nearly perfect. The Royals are coming into game 1 of Players Weekend off a 3–2 loss at home versus the Rockies. Kansas City scored their second and final run in the second inning against the Rockies but could not buy a run for the remaining seven innings in the loss. The Royals are in third place in the AL-Central, with a record of 64–62, 6-games behind the first place Indians. The starting pitcher for the Indians in game 1 is the twenty-five-year-old Ryan Merritt. The young man would pitch six and two-thirds innings of shutout baseball, striking out three batters. In the top of the first inning, Merritt is pitching to the Royals' right fielder, Melky Cabrera, with one out and Lorenzo Cain on first, who reached base on a fielder's choice force out at third. Merritt's 1–2 pitch to Cabrera gets chopped on the ground in the hole, with a diving grab and glove flip by shortstop Frankie Lindor to Ramírez covering second who fires the ball to first baseman, Carlos Santana, for an inning ending double play!

The Royals fail to score, and now Cleveland looks to make some noise with their first at bat. But the game stays scoreless as we move along into the third inning. In the bottom of the third, the Indians' third baseman, Giovanny "Gio" Urshela, is facing the Royals' starter, Jason Vargas. Urshela is batting with zero out and Yan Gomes on base with a leadoff single that hit off the wall in right field. Vargas's slings his first pitch to Urshela, and he hits a ball deep to left field. That ball hits off the wall and beyond the reach of left fielder Alex Gordon, who makes a leaping grab attempt against the wall. Gomes scores all the way from first on the RBI double by Giovanny Urshela, giving the Tribe an early 1–0 lead over Kansas City. Ryan Merritt has pitched a full five innings with two strikeouts and has kept Kansas City from scoring, thanks to some hard work from his defense.

The Royals have had some scoring chances, but Merritt has kept all three base runners stranded. In the bottom of the fifth inning, the Indians are batting with a two-run lead, and their shortstop, Francisco "Mr. Smile" Lindor, is batting with one out and Urshela on first. Urshela lined a single-to-center field after Yan Gomes struck out swinging. Francisco Lindor is 0–2 today, facing Vargas with a groundout in the third inning. Lindor has the count in his favor, 3–0, Vargas makes his eighty-sixth pitch of the game.

"Lindor launches it deep left into the bleachers, a two-run homer for Mr. Smile! It's 4-0 Indians, home run number 23 for Lindor. On a weekend where players are encouraged to have some fun, nobody has more on a regular basis than Lindor," Matt Underwood said.

As we move to the top of the ninth, Indian's closer, Cody Allen, stays in the game to pitch in a nonsave situation. Allen replaced Tyler Olson with two out in the top of the eighth inning. The first two Royals have been set down—Jorge Bonifacio struck out swinging and Alcides Escobar popped out to Ramírez at second base. Now, third baseman, Cheslor Cuthbert, steps in. The 0–2 pitch, "A swing and a miss ball game! He chased the high heat, and Cody Allen finishes with a flourish, and the Indians have pitched their league, leading thirteenth shutout of the year, started by Ryan Merritt" Tom Hamilton says. The Indians win the Players Weekend opener by a final score of 4–0. Ryan Merritt wins his first game of the season in his first start, and Kansas City falls to 64–63 on the year, now seven games behind the Indians in the Central Division. Cleveland improves their record to 71–56.

Players Weekend continues in Cleveland as the Indians host game 2 against the Kansas City Royals. The Indians have taken a 1–0 series lead, with a 4–0 shutout victory pitched in game 1 on Friday night. Tonight's first pitch is at 7:12 pm, and tonight's game calls for "Sunshine." Indian's pitcher, Mike Clevinger, gets the start, and he is looking to pitch a better ball game than his previous starts. In his last two appearances, one as a relief pitcher on August 17, Clevinger gave up two earned runs and a go-ahead home run hit by Max Kepler late in the game in Minnesota. The Tribe fell short and took a 4–2 loss to the Twins on Aug 17. Clevinger took his fifth loss of the campaign, and the Indians' record dropped to 66–53.

Four days later, on August 21, Mike Clevinger got the start against the Red Sox. Clevinger surrendered two more home runs for a total of four earned runs pitching for four and one-third innings.

The Indians beat the Red Sox, 5–4, but Clevinger took a no-decision. Today Cleveland is looking to get a stronger start from their young starter. The Royals are in a scoreless tie with the Tribe in the top of the fifth inning. Mike "Sunshine" Clevinger is pitching to Kansas City's center fielder, Lorenzo Cain, with two out and Whit Merrifield on base. Merrifield reached base on a ground ball that wasn't fielded cleanly by Francisco Lindor, giving the Royals an extra out in this inning. Cain is searching for a clutch two-strike hit to score Merrifield and give Kansas City a lead in the middle innings. Mike Clevinger winds up for his eighty-sixth pitch of the game, and Cain "swung on line-drive left-center field long run Zimmer leaps. Did he make the catch? Oh, he did! Another highlight-reel catch by Bradley Zimmer! The only way this game is still scoreless, is because Zimmer played Superman again," Jim Rosenhaus said. Machine is his nickname, and speed is his game. What a grab by Zimmer, stretching out as far as he could to catch it!

We move to the bottom half of the fifth, and the Cleveland Indians have made some great plays defensively through the first five innings. Clevinger has already struck out seven Royal's batters, and thanks to Zimmer's run saving grab, the Indians will look to score first. Kansas City's starter, Jason Hammel, continues to pitch well into the bottom of the fifth inning as he kept the Indians off the scoreboard. Indians' hitters are again retired in order. Edwin Encarnacion, Jay Bruce, and Carlos Santana all hit into flyouts. Two of the three balls were caught by the Royals' right fielder, Melky Cabrera, and Jason Hammel maintains a perfect game through the first five innings. Mike Clevinger heads back out for his sixth inning of work, keeping the Royals from scoring for a sixth consecutive inning and striking out Eric Hosmer and Salvador Perez. The designated hitter, Mike Moustakas, grounds out to Tribe's second baseman, José Ramírez, and Kansas City leaves a runner stranded at first base.

The Indians are batting in the bottom of the sixth inning, and Yandy Díaz leads off the inning grounding out sharply back to the mound. Jason Hammel fires the ball over to first baseman Hosmer for the first out. Sixteen consecutive batters retired by Hammel, who also has four strikeouts. The Indians' center fielder, Bradley Zimmer, breaks up Hammel's perfect game with a one-out single punched into center field. In the top of the fifth inning, Zimmer made the amazing leaping grab that saved a run and kept the game scoreless, now, he is Cleveland's first base runner and he's got speed. The Indians' catcher, Roberto Pérez, steps up to the plate with the go-ahead run on base. Pérez is 0–1 in the game with a swinging strikeout that ended the third inning. Hammel offers the 0–1 pitch, Pérez hits the ball to deep left center field high off the railing above the wall, and the umpires say it's a two-run homer for Roberto "Bebo" Pérez! Perez hits just his third home run on the year, but it's a big one, as it gives the Indians a 2–0 lead with one out in the sixth inning. The Indians can't add to their lead but are ahead of the Royals by two as we go to the top of the seventh inning.

The Indians' manager, Terry Francona, decides to make a pitching change to start the inning, and relief pitcher, Bryan Shaw, replaces starter Mike Clevinger, who pitched six shutout innings with a new career high of nine strikeouts. Clevinger has given the Indians the start they had hoped for, and he is in position to win his seventh game. Shaw makes quick work of the Royals with a "three up, three down" seventh inning. Alcides Escobar and Alex Gordon both hit into groundouts, and Bryan Shaw gets the third baseman, Cheslor Cuthbert, on a swinging strikeout. Once again, the Royals can't find a way to score, this time facing the Indians bullpen. Jason Hammel is sent back out to pitch the bottom of the seventh inning for Kansas City, and his team trails the Indians, 2–0. Edwin Encarnacion leads off the inning, he is 0–2, with a strikeout and a flyout. Hammel makes his first pitch, and on one swing, Encarnacion makes it a 3–0 game with a solo home run blasted above the nineteen-foot wall to the bleachers in left. Home run number 30 for Edwin "EE" Encarnacion and RBI number 75 as he does his signature "walk the parrot" around the bases and becomes the first player in MLB history to homer thirty times in six straight seasons. This is his first season with the Indians, and that is the second straight inning that Jason Hammel has allowed a home run.

Jay Bruce is retired for the first out as Hammel gets Bruce to ground out to the Royals' second baseman, Whit Merrifield. Bruce is now 0–3, facing Hammel tonight. Now there's one out, and Carlos Santana steps in for his third at bat of the game. Santana is 0–2 with a flyout to Cabrera in right field his last plate appearance. Santana is a very patient hitter, and he is waiting for Jason Hammel to make his 1–0 pitch. Carlos "Slamtana" Santana swings and smokes a line drive solo home run down the right field line above the nine foot wall. That ball got out of here in a hurry! Cleveland goes up 4–0 on Santana's nineteenth home run of the season! The Tribe didn't have a single base runner until one out in the sixth inning, and now Cleveland is leading by a big margin, thanks to three home runs surrendered by Hammel in the past two innings. In the top of the ninth inning, the Indians' closer, Cody Allen, comes on to replace Dan Otero in a nonsave situation. Eric Hosmer is on second, and Alcides Escobar is at the plate.

"The 0–2 pitch, swing, and a pop-up first base side foul ground Santana near the Royals dugout, leans over the railing makes the catch, ball game!" Tom Hamilton says.

The Royals drop the second game off MLB Players Weekend as the Cleveland Indians win, 4–0, for the second night in a row! The Indians get their league leading fourteenth shutout of the season, fifth time this year the Indians have shut out the Kansas City Royals. Mike Clevinger wins his seventh game of the season with his strong outing of six scoreless innings and new career high with nine strikeouts. The Indians will play for a three-game sweep tomorrow afternoon, with the first pitch at 1:10 p.m.

On a weekend where players are encouraged to have some fun with their new uniforms, the Indians are doing that and more. Cleveland has taken the first two games of this Players Weekend series, winning both games by a score of 4–0, already securing a series win. In yesterday's game, the Tribe scored all four of their runs off the home run ball after Jason Hammel was perfect for five and one-third innings. The starting pitching in the first two games has been phenomenal for Cleveland. Ryan Merritt and Mike Clevinger have combined for a total of twelve and two-thirds innings with twelve strikeouts and giving up zero runs against the Royals. Carlos "Cookie" Carrasco gets the start in this third and final game of the

Players Weekend series for the Indians. In his last start against Boston on August 22, Carrasco allowed six of the nine runs given up by the Indians in six and two-thirds innings, while his teammates gave him very little run support. The Indians took a 9–1 loss, getting no more than one hit off a leadoff home run by Francisco Lindor to begin the bottom of the first inning.

For this series' finale, second baseman, Whit Merrifield, leads off the top of the first inning for Kansas City, and Carlos Carrasco makes quick work of the Royals by sending them back to the dugout in order. Merrifield pops out to the Indians' second baseman, José Ramírez. Center Fielder Lorenzo Cain grounded out to third baseman, Yandy Díaz, and Eric Hosmer is Carrasco's first strikeout victim. With the Royals sent down in order, the Indians will look to provide some run support for their starter. The starting pitcher for Kansas City is left hander Eric Skoglund. The Royals' pitching has had trouble in games 1 and 2 facing the Indians, allowing four home runs in the first two ball games. Today Skoglund will look to silence the Indians' bats with a strong start on the mound. The leadoff hitter for the Indians in the bottom of the first inning is shortstop, Francisco Lindor, who reaches base on a leadoff walk. With Lindor on first base, left fielder Austin "A Jax" Jackson steps up for his first at bat, and Jackson quickly gets aboard on Skoglund's second pitch as he singles a sharp line drive to left fielder Alex Gordon while Frankie Lindor holds up at second base.

In the early stages of this ball game, the Indians are threatening to score first with two men on base as José Ramírez, the league leader in extra base hits, steps up to bat with nobody out and a golden opportunity to give the Tribe an early first inning lead. With a 1–0 count, Skoglund makes his pitch to Ramírez. José smacks the ball fair down the third baseline and into left field, and the ball kicks up against the sidewall for a double. Lindor jogs home from second to give the Indians a 1–0 lead in the first inning, and Austin Jackson stays put at third base. José Ramírez slugs his forty-first double of the season, and RBI number 60 and the Indians still have nobody out. The Royals' starter is in an early jam with two men on base and zero out, and Cleveland is already out in front by a run. The Tribe's designated hitter, Edwin Encarnacion, comes to bat; he went 1–4 yesterday, hitting a solo home run off Jason Hammel. The Royals' pitcher, Eric Skoglund, gets ahead of Encarnacion with a one-ball, two-strike count, and Skoglund makes his sixteenth pitch of the inning. Edwin swings and grounds out to the second baseman, Whit Merrifield, who retires him at first, but Jackson scores from third base on the out.

A productive first out by Encarnacion not only puts the Indians up, 2–0, but also advances José Ramírez from second to third base. Encarnacion gets his seventy-sixth RBI on the year. Indians' first baseman, Carlos Santana, is unable to score Ramírez from third base as he pops out to first baseman, Eric Hosmer, in foul territory for the second out. Right fielder Brandon Guyer steps in, looking to lend a hand to his teammate. Guyer is down to his last strike, and Skoglund is looking to end the inning with just a small amount of damage. As Guyer takes the 2–2 pitch, he swings and chops the ball on the ground and in the hole beyond the infielder's reach into left field for an RBI single. José Ramírez scores from third, and Guyer's two-out single into left plates a third run! He got just enough bat on that low pitch, what clutch hitting by Brandon "BG" Guyer! It's a three-run first inning for the Indians, as they have taken advantage of some early scoring chances. The inning ends on a swinging strikeout by Bradley Zimmer as Carlos Carrasco trots back to the mound in the top of the second inning with a comfortable 3–0 lead. In the top of the second inning, the Royals look to cut into the Indian's lead as Melky Cabrera led off the second inning with a double that's smoked into left field for his twenty-second double on the season.

Now the designated hitter, Mike Moustakas, will try and get the Royals on the board. Moustakas falls behind Carrasco with a one-ball, two-strike count, and Cookie's next pitch is swung on and missed! Moustakas chases the high heat above the shoulders for strike three! The Royals' third baseman has no answer as Cuthbert strikes out on three pitches. Two consecutive strikeouts for Carrasco keeps Cabrera on second base with two down, and Alcides Escobar is batting fourth in the inning. Escobar is looking to extend the inning for the Royals and score Melky Cabrera from second the pitch, and

Escobar skies the ball on the infield. Francisco Lindor makes the grab, and the inning is over. Carlos Carrasco recovers quickly from the leadoff double that he surrendered, and he adds two more strikeouts to his total, giving him three in the first two innings. The Royals leave a runner stranded in scoring position, and the Indians are coming to bat. Yan Gomes will lead off the bottom of the second for the Indians. Gomes is batting in the ninth spot, and he reaches base with a leadoff single hit to Alex Gordon in left. Now the lineup flips to the leadoff spot with Francisco Lindor, who is 0–0 with a walk, and a run scored.

"Now the 1–2, swung on blasted, deep left center field it is gone! A two-run missile over the nineteen-foot wall in left center," Tom Hamilton says.

Lindor's twenty-fourth home run gives the Indians a 5–0 lead, and they are grand slam proof. The next batter, Austin Jackson, reaches base off Eric Skoglund as he smokes a double into left field as the ball skips beyond Gordon and all the way to the wall. Jackson is now two for two with a double and a single, and he has scored once. The Royals' manager, Ned Yost, saunters to the mound for a visit, as his pitcher has been unable to set down the first three Cleveland batters. With the game back underway, the Royals' defense records out number one as José Ramírez pops out to the second baseman, Whit Merrifield. Following the flyout, the Indians' designated hitter, Edwin Encarnacion, reaches base with a one out walk. Jackson moves up to second base, and the Indians have two men on with one out as Carlos Santana steps in for his second at bat. Santana is 0–1 with a pop out to Hosmer in foul ground.

Seeing enough, the Royals make a pitching change. Onelki Garcia replaces starter Eric Skoglund with two men on and one out. Skoglund is responsible for the two base runners, Jackson and Encarnacion. Early in the at bat, Onelki Garcia make his second pitch to Santana.

"The pitch, swung on blasted deep left, down the line off the foul pole, three-run homer! So number 20 for Carlos Santana. It's official, it's a rout! It's 8–0 Indians in the second inning, and Santana nearly knocked over the foul pole," Tom Hamilton says.

That officially ends Eric Skoglund's day, and he pitched one and one-third innings, allowing seven runs. The Royals' relief pitcher continues to struggle getting men out as the next three batters reach base. Brandon Guyer singles on a ground ball to second base and then advances to second on a throwing error by Whit Merrifield. The play is recorded as a hit and an error, and Guyer is 2–2 with an RBI. Yandy Díaz remains 1–1 as he reaches base with a free pass issued by Onelki Garcia. The Indians' center fielder, Bradley Zimmer, gets an infield single on a ball hit to the second baseman, Merrifield, who drops the baseball as he tried to make the play. It's an infield single, and everybody is safe. Now the Indians have the bases loaded, Guyer on third, Díaz on second, and Zimmer on first. Yan Gomes is batting with one out, and Gomes started the inning with a leadoff single to left and came home to score on Lindor's two-run home run. Gomes takes the first pitch for a strike. The Indians are sitting on an 8–0 lead and have homered twice in this inning.

"The pitch swung on blasted to deep left awwaaaay back and gone! Yan Gomes has hit the Indian's fifth grand slam, and the Indians have removed, if there was any doubt, leading it, 12–0. A nine-run second inning and there is still only one out," Tom Hamilton says.

A season-high nine runs in an inning for the Tribe as Yan "Gomer" Gomes produces Cleveland's third home run of this inning, and the Tribe is now leading Kansas City, 12–0. This grand slam is the Indians' fifth on the season. In 2016, although the Tribe had many long balls, none were a grand slam. It's now the top of the ninth inning with two outs, with the Wahoos in command, leading the Kansas City Royals by a dozen runs. Zach "Z-Mac" McAllister is just the second relief pitcher in this game for Cleveland.

"Now the 1–0 pitch. A swing and a fly ball to left field, Jackson's camped under it he makes the catch, ball game! What a weekend for the Tribe! They cap it off with a 12–0 demolition job of the Royals and sweep Kansas City and shut them out all three times," Tom Hamilton adds.

The Indians decided this game early, scoring all twelve-runs in just the first two innings. Kansas City has set a franchise record going thirty-four consecutive innings without producing a run. Before coming to Cleveland, they were shut out in the last seven innings of game three versus the Colorado Rockies, and now Cleveland's pitching staff blanked the Royals for an entire weekend series. Carlos Carrasco gets win number 13, striking out eight Royal's batters in seven innings. In this three-game Player Weekend series, the Indians outscored the Kansas City Royals, 20–0. Fifteen of the twenty runs came off seven home run balls, and Francisco Lindor and Carlos Santana both went deep twice. The Indians will now leave Cleveland for an eleven-game road trip, traveling to three different cities before returning home on September 8.

Chapter 2

Brooms in the Bronx, Games 5–7

August 28 starts an eleven-game road trip for the Indians, beginning with a three-game series against the New York Yankees at Yankee Stadium. The Yankees came to Cleveland on August 3 and split a four-game series with the Tribe winning games 1 and 2. The Indians come into game 1 on a four-game win streak, outscoring their opponents by a score of 33–6! The Indians beat their Central Division rivals, shutting out the Royals, 12–0, on August 27. The Indians lost to New York, 8–1, on August 6 when Carlos Carrasco took the loss, allowing five runs in five and two-thirds innings pitched. The Yankees begin this series with a record of 70–59, just two and a half games behind the Boston Red Sox. New York is coming off a two-games-to-one-series victory over the Seattle Mariners, winning the last game, 10–1.

Pitching in game 1 for the Yankees is the Cy Young candidate, Luis Severino, who begins this game with a record of 11–5 and an ERA below four. Severino quickly gets the first two outs, the leadoff, hitter Francisco, Lindor grounds out to the first baseman, Greg Bird, and the left fielder, Austin Jackson, gets called out on strikes. With the first two batters retired, José Ramírez, the league leader in extra base hits, steps up for his first at bat. Severino checks the signs from his catcher, Gary Sánchez, as he prepares to offer the 3–2 pitch to Ramírez.

"The payoff swung on. This is hit a ton to deep right center, and it is gone! José Ramírez with a solo homer to right center, his nineteenth," Tom Hamilton says.

Just like that, the Indians take a 1–0 lead over the Yankees in the top of the first. The designated hitter, Edwin Encarnacion, grounds out to the second baseman, Starlin Castro, for the third out, and the side is retired. The Indians quickly get to Severino as José Ramírez gives the Indians a 1–0 lead with a solo home run. We go to the bottom of the first inning, and the Indians hand the baseball to arguably the best starting pitcher in the American League and maybe in all of baseball. Corey Kluber starts this game with a 12–4 record and a 2.65 ERA. The Yankee's left fielder, Brett Gardner, grabs a bat for New York, hitting leadoff in the bottom of the first inning with his team trailing by a run. Gardner gets sent back to the dugout on a ground ball hit to the second baseman, José Ramírez, for out number 1. Kluber makes quick work of the Yankees with a three-up-three-down first inning as the right fielder, Aaron Hicks, strikes out swinging, and Kluber has Gary Sánchez guessing as he is struck out looking for out number 3. Corey Kluber looks sharp in the bottom of the first with two strikeouts.

Next up, Jay Bruce will lead off for the Indians in the top of the second inning. Bruce is batting fifth in Terry Francona's lineup, and the Indians are in front of the Yankees, 1–0, after one inning. Severino delivers the pitch, and Bruce swings and grounds out to Todd Frazier at third base for the first out. First baseman, Carlos Santana, grounds out to the Yankee's first baseman, Greg Bird, and Luis Severino gets Bradley Zimmer to strike out, swinging for his second strikeout of the game. Corey Kluber heads back to the mound for the bottom of the second inning. The Yankees' shortstop, Didi Gregorius, is batting in the cleanup spot for manager Joe Girardi. Gregorius is set down on a flyout to the center fielder, Bradley Zimmer, for out number 1. The Yankees' second baseman, Starlin Castro, is retired for the second out as he grounds out to the Indians' second baseman, José Ramírez. With two out and no men on base, first baseman, Greg Bird, steps into the batter's box for his first at bat against Kluber. Bird is down to his last strike, and the toss-and-strike three is called! Corey

Kluber, the American League Cy Young candidate, has set down the first six Yankee batters, three via the strikeout!

New York is batting in the bottom of the third inning, and the Indians have been set down in order for a second straight inning. Luis Severino gets Francisco Lindor to chase a pitch, and Lindor strikes out for the third out. Severino now has his third strikeout of the game. Chase Headley, the Yankees' designated hitter, makes some noise for New York as Kluber gives up a solo home run blast to right field to tie the game at 1–1 to start the bottom of the third inning. Headley hits his ninth homer of the season, and the Yankees' bats are warming up. Corey Kluber regains his composure as he retires the next three Yankee batters. The center fielder, Jacoby Ellsbury, lines out to Austin Jackson in left field. Third baseman, Todd Frazier, strikes out swinging, giving Kluber four strikeouts on the day. The lineup goes back to the top of the order with Brett Gardner, who is 0–1 today with a groundout to Ramírez. The first pitch to Gardner is swung on, and he lines a ball into the glove of the diving first baseman, Carlos Santana! That ball was headed to right field, and Brett Gardner gets robbed of a base hit by Santana on a diving grab for the third out! Kluber surrenders a home run, and the Yankees have tied the game at one as we go to the top of the fourth inning.

The leadoff hitter for Cleveland in the top of the fourth is Austin Jackson, and for the second at bat in a row, he gets fanned by Luis Severino, chasing ball 4 in the dirt. With one out, José Ramírez steps in for his second at bat. Ramírez is Cleveland's only base runner, if you include the fact he never stayed on base. He came home to score on a solo home run in the first inning. Ramírez strolls to first base with one out on the first walk issued by Luis Severino. Now the designated hitter, Edwin Encarnacion, is batting with Ramírez on first, the pitch, and Ramírez breaks for second; the throw by Sánchez is not in time! That is the fourteenth stolen base by the Indians' second baseman, and now Encarnacion is batting with the go-ahead run standing on second. Edwin Encarnacion looks to bring home Ramírez with a one out hit, the 2–2 pitch, and Ramírez sprints toward third. The pitch is called ball 3, and Yankees' catcher, Gary Sánchez, launches a bullet and throws Ramirez out, trying to steal third. The tag was applied by third baseman, Todd Frazier, and the Yankees' defense eliminates the Tribe's go-ahead base runner for out number 2. Severino issues his second and third walk of the inning, and Encarnacion and Bruce are now on base with two out and Santana at the plate. Carlos Santana swings away with two men on, and he falls behind, 0–1. On Severino's next offering, Santana yanks this ball over the line but foul. If that ball stayed fair, the Indians would have regained the lead. It's a 0–2 count, and Santana is caught looking for strike 3, and the Indians leave both runners stranded. Strikeout number five for Severino, who has only allowed one run.

New York is batting in the bottom of the fifth inning, and batters 6, 7, and 8 will face Kluber, who through four innings has struck out five batters and has given up a run on a solo dinger hit by Chase Headley. Corey Kluber sets down Bird and Headley, but Jacoby Ellsbury keeps the inning going with a two-out double to left field, his twelfth double on the season. Todd Frazier smacks an RBI single into left, and Ellsbury scores from second base, and New York moves out in front to take a 2–1 lead in the bottom of the fifth. Kluber was moving quickly in this inning, but now he's going to need to put in a little more work to try and get Brett Gardner for the third out. Kluber has Gardner down, 1–2; the pitch and strike 3 is called! A fastball right over the plate and Gardner took it! Kluber gets his sixth strikeout of the game, but the Yankees do take a 2–1 lead with a two out single to left by Todd Frazier. The Indians trail the Yankees by a run at the end of five innings.

In the top of the sixth inning, two men are out, and the bases are empty for the Tribe. Luis Severino gets strikeouts 7 and 8 as Lindor and Jackson both remain without a hit. The second baseman, José Ramírez, is 1–1 with a homer and a walk in the fourth inning. Severino winds up.

"The pitch, swung on blasted deep right field way up and outta here into the second deck! José Ramírez, two, New York, two. Boy, did he put a charge into that baby!" Tom Hamilton says.

Yes, Ramírez has his second solo home run, and he has tied the game at two! Home run number 20 for Ramírez as he brings this game back even with a no-doubt-about-it blast to the upper deck.

This game is tied at two as we go to the bottom of inning number 6; Corey Kluber comes back on the hill to pitch and has struck out six batters and allowed a solo homer by Chase Headley and a two out RBI single to Todd Frazier. The right fielder, Aaron Hicks, is next and is 0–2 today; Kluber has struck Hicks out both times. Kluber issues his first walk of the game as he walks Hicks on five pitches, and the Yankees have a leadoff base runner. Aaron Hicks represents the go-ahead run in this tie ball game, but he is left stranded as Kluber sets down Gary Sánchez, Didi Gregorius, and Starlin Castro in order. The three Yankee batters all fly out to end inning number 6, and Cleveland's batters 5, 6, and 7 will bat in the top of the seventh inning of a tie ball game.

Jay Bruce will face Severino for a third time, and Bruce is 0–1 with a groundout and a walk in the fourth inning. Bruce comes up empty as he grounds out to Starlin Castro at second base, giving the Tribe their initial out. The Indians' first baseman, Carlos Santana, steps up to the plate; Santana is hitless so far today, and this is his third at bat. Luis Severino caught Santana looking in his previous at bat to end the top of the fourth inning. So far, José Ramírez has been the only sign of life offensively for the Indians with two home runs. Carlos Santana awaits the 1–1 pitch from Severino, and now he calls time and steps out of the batter's box. Santana climbs back in and now the pitch.

"Santana with a drive, deep to right, there she goes, into the second deck! A laser off the bat of Santana, and the Indians have a three-to-two lead in the seventh. They have three hits tonight, they have three home runs," Tom Hamilton says.

Next up for the Indians is center fielder Bradley Zimmer, who smokes his first hit with a one out single lined to Ellsbury in center field. Yan Gomes strikes out for out number two, and Severino will try to retire Giovanny Urshela and keep Zimmer stranded at first base. The Yankees have Adam Warren warming up in the bullpen, and Joe Girardi makes the call and brings him in. Luis Severino leaves the game, allowing three earned runs off three solo home runs in six and two-thirds innings pitched. As Warren's 0–1 pitch is made to Urshela, Zimmer sprints toward second, and he is safe! Zimmer leaps up and hustles to third as the ball got away from Starlin Castro on the throw from Gary Sánchez and made its way into centerfield. The 1–1 pitch by Warren gets away from Sánchez and ricochets to the backstop as Zimmer scores from third. The Indians now lead the Yankees, 4–2, on pure hustle by Zimmer. Greg Bird leads off the bottom of the seventh inning for the Yankees, 0-2, facing the Indian's ace. Corey Kluber struck out Bird to end the second inning, and now Bird is down in the count, 0–2. The pitch by Kluber and strike 3 called! Strikeout number 7 for Kluber as he gets Greg Bird looking at a breaking ball on the outer half of the plate. A well-placed off-speed pitch by Kluber for the first out.

Chase Headley and Jacoby Ellsbury both hit into groundouts to the Tribe's Ramírez, and the side is retired. As the Indians come to bat in the eighth, they are leading the New York Yankees, 4–2. New York's Warren retires Francisco Lindor on a groundout that was hit to Greg Bird at first base. Lindor is now 0–4 with two groundouts and two strikeouts. Austin Jackson now bats, and as Adam Warren makes his 3–2 pitch, Jackson swings and drives this ball to deep left field. This ball is on its way…and gone! Jackson's sixth home run puts the Tribe up by three, but the Yankees have the play reviewed, and the replay crew here in New York says it's a home run. A fan may have interfered with the ball, and it was unclear for sure if the ball cleared the wall, but the call stands. At 5-2, the Indians have hit four solo home runs tonight! The Indians take a three-run lead into the bottom of the eighth, and Jackson's home run gives Kluber a little more room for error.

In the bottom of the eighth, the Yankees' bats are silenced again by Kluber, a three-up, three-down inning. The Yankees have only reached base once with a hit in their last eleven at bats, and the Yankees' only other base runner came on Cory Kluber's only walk in the sixth inning. Corey Kluber has kept New York off the scoreboard since Frazier's RBI single that scored Jacoby Ellsbury to put them in the lead by a run in the fifth inning. It's the top of the ninth inning, and pitcher Chasen Shreve replaces Adam Warren with his team down, 5–2. Jay Bruce is out number 1 as Shreve gets him to swing and miss on three straight pitches. With one out, Carlos Santana is batting for the fourth time in this game. Santana gave the Indians a 3–2 lead with his solo home run in the top of the seventh inning. The Indians added one more run with a wild pitch that scored Bradley Zimmer from third base with two outs. Carlos Santana gets walked, that is the fourth walk allowed by Yankee pitching in this ball game. Bradley Zimmer, now batting, he is 1–3 with a single and two strike-outs. Chasen Shreve makes the first pitch to Zimmer.

"A swing and a line shot to center field, it's a base hit. It will get down and get by everybody and go to the wall in center. That will score Santana from first, and stopping at second with an RBI double is Bradley Zimmer," Tom Hamilton says.

The Indians extended their lead to four, now leading the Yankees, 6–2, as we go to the bottom of the ninth inning. Cody Allen comes on to replace starter Corey Kluber, who pitches eight innings and gives up only two runs and strikes out seven. Kluber is in position to get his thirteenth win, with Allen pitching to Starlin Castro with two out and the bases empty.

"Now the 1–2 pitch, curveball swung on and missed, ball game! So the Cleveland Indians get a quick one, two, three inning from Cody Allen, and he finishes off another strong Indians outing with a strikeout of Starlin Castro, and the Indians are a 6–2 winner over the Yankees to start this eleven-game road trip," Tom Hamilton says.

Teams can't play ball when it rains, and on August 29, Mother Nature just wouldn't cooperate with the Indians and the Yankees. Game 2 of this three-game series in New York gets called due to heavy rainfall that lasted for most of the day. The Indians aren't scheduled to return to New York, so both ball clubs agree to play the final two games in a doubleheader on August 30, the next day. The Indians and the Yankees are getting ready for game 1 of this day/night dou-bleheader, and the first pitch is set for 1:05 p.m. The weather for game 1 is seventy-four degrees and sunny with the wind blowing out to right field. The Indians won the first game on Monday against the Yankees by a score of 6–2, with four long balls by the Tribe, two hit by José Ramírez.

Corey Kluber won his thirteenth game and strikes out seven batters in eight innings. Monday's starter for New York, Luis

Severino, takes the loss, allowing three home runs in six and two-thirds innings, and Severino's record falls to 11–6. The starting pitcher today for the Yankees is the lefty Jaime García with a record of five wins and eight losses. The Yankees come into today's game with a team record of 70–60, and the Indians are 74–56, having won five in a row. As the shortstop, Francisco Lindor, steps up to lead off game 1 of this day/night doubleheader, fans are still entering the park on the first pitch that gets called for strike 1, and we are underway in the Bronx. Francisco Lindor had an unusually quiet game yesterday, going 0–4 with two strikeouts and two groundouts facing Severino. The lefthander García throws his 0–1 pitch, and Lindor swings and lines the ball in the right field gap between Aaron Hicks and Jacoby Ellsbury for a leadoff base hit. Brandon Guyer is the starting left fielder for the Indians in game 1 of this doubleheader and bats second. Guyer's last game was on Sunday, August 27, when he tallied three hits and an RBI in the 12–0 win over the Royals. Guyer becomes out number one as he hits a fly ball to center fielder Jacoby Ellsbury who makes the grab, and Lindor is unable to move into scoring position.

The second baseman, José Ramírez, is batting third in the lineup for Terry Francona, and in Monday night's win, Ramírez went 2–3 with two solo home runs, both coming with two outs against Luis Severino. Ramírez falls behind in the count with one ball and two strikes against García. On the next pitch, Lindor flies toward second base, and the pitch is high for ball 2. Sánchez throws to second, and Lindor is in safely with a feet first slide. Francisco Lindor nabs stolen base number 11, and Cleveland has a good opportunity to score early against García with Lindor advancing to second on the steal. García takes the sign from Gary Sánchez, and the 2–2 pitch to Ramírez is swung on and chopped in the hole by the diving Didi Gregorius and into left field for a base hit. Lindor stops at third, and the Indians have runners at the corners with one out and Yandy Díaz coming to bat. Francisco Lindor represents the go-ahead run in this scoreless game, as he is ninety feet from home plate. If Díaz can avoid hitting into a double play, Cleveland should be able to score.

With the "infield back the pitch, and it gets away from Sánchez, here comes Lindor, and the Indians have a 1–0 lead, and Gary Sánchez continues to botch pitches" comments Tom Hamilton.

The Indians get a gift run on the passed ball by Gary Sánchez, and Lindor scores the first run for the Indians, and José Ramírez moves to second base with one out. Jaime García's next pitch is low for ball 2, and it's a 2–0 count for Díaz. The pitch is delivered, and Yandy Díaz swings and grounds the ball past the diving infield and into center field. Ramírez rounds third and scores on the one-out RBI single, and it's an early two-run lead for the Indians. Edwin Encarnacion is sitting out for game 1 of this doubleheader, and Díaz is assigned to the designated hitter position and gets the job done. It's a 2–0 Tribe lead, and García has only thrown eleven pitches. Jay Bruce is the fifth man to bat in the first inning, and Bruce gets fanned by García for the second out. Carlos Santana is retired on a pop-out to the second baseman, Ronald Torreyes, to end the inning. The Indians score twice in the top half of the first against Jaime García, and one run was unearned.

As we move ahead to the bottom of the third inning, the Indians are leading the Yankees, 2–0. The Tribe's starting hurler, Trevor Bauer, gets his first strikeout against Brett Gardner as he foul-tipped the ball into the glove of Roberto Pérez to begin the bottom half of the inning. The Yankees' right fielder, Aaron Hicks, got aboard with a one-out walk, as Bauer couldn't get Hicks to chase the 3–2 breaking ball below his knees. The Yankees' trail, 2–0, and Gary Sánchez is 0–1 today with a flyout to the center fielder, Bradley Zimmer, in the bottom of the first inning. Hicks is on first base, and Bauer slipped into motion the pitch, and Sánchez hits a sharp grounder to Lindor at short, who makes a diving backhanded stop, springs up, and throws to Santana for the second out! The ball bounces to first base on the throw by Lindor, and Carlos Santana scoops the ball into his glove for the out. A strong defensive play on both ends as Aaron Hicks moves up to second, but the Yankees have two outs.

Didi Gregorius comes to bat, and Trevor Bauer takes the sign from Roberto Pérez, first pitch, and it gets by Perez to the backstop as Aaron Hicks jogs to third base. There are two out for Gregorius, with the Indians leading the Yankees, 2–0, in the third inning. The next pitch on a 3–1 count by Bauer, and Gregorius hits a sharp drive near the third base line that falls into left field for an RBI double. Aaron Hicks scores without a throw, and it's a 2–1 ball game with the Tribe holding to a precarious lead. First baseman Chase Headley is batting with two out; the Tribe in front by a run as the lead was just cut in half on the two out double to left by Gregorius. The pitch by Bauer, and he throws the ball away again. Gregorius rumbles to third, and the Yankees have the tying run just ninety feet from home plate. Headley is batting with two strikes, and the Yankees are unable to tie this game as Trevor Bauer ends the third inning with a swinging strikeout. Chase Headley waves at a heater in the dirt, and Bauer gets out of a jam with his second strikeout.

At 2–1, Indians move ahead to the bottom of the ninth inning. The Indians' closer, Cody Allen, replaced Bryan Shaw with two out in the Yankees' eighth inning. Shaw struck out Chase Headley, and he retired Didi Gregorius on a line out to Giovanny Urshela at the hot corner. Cody Allen is searching for a four-out save, with the Tribe still leading the Yankees, 2–1. The Yankee's manager, Joe Girardi, replaces third baseman, Todd Frazier, with pinch hitter Starlin Castro. Allen moves ahead in the count one ball, two strikes, and the fourth pitch to Castro is swung on and missed! Castro, on a half swing, goes too far and can't hold up for out number one. Jacoby Ellsbury bats next, and he is 0–3, grounding out two times. Allen offers his first pitch, and Ellsbury hits a ground ball right at Giovanny Urshela at third. Urshela scoops the ball into his glove and throws out Ellsbury for the second out. The Yankees still trail the Indians by a run, and a second pinch hitter, Aaron Judge, will replace second baseman, Ronald Torreyes. The rookie power hitter is the Yankees' last hope as New York trails by a run with two down in the bottom of the ninth. Judge is very capable of tying this game with a long ball, and he is making Allen work, now batting with a full count.

"Here's the payoff pitch from Allen, swing and a miss, ball game! It was the high heat from Cody Allen, and he struck out Aaron Judge to end the ball game. What a job today by Trevor Bauer, Tyler Olson, Bryan Shaw, and Cody Allen," comments Tom Hamilton.

From Yankee Stadium in The Bronx, New York, the Yankees and the Indians are just about ready to start game two of this day/night doubleheader. The Indians have won the first two games of this eleven-game road trip with a 6–2 win on Monday night and a 2–1 win earlier this afternoon in game one of the doubleheader. Earlier today, the Indians scored both runs in the top of the first inning in game one, and terrific pitching by Trevor Bauer and the Tribe bullpen kept the Yankee lineup at bay. Bauer won his fourteenth game pitching six innings and allowing one run. The Tribe's closer, Cody Allen, earned save number 22 with two strikeouts in the ninth inning. The Yankees come into game two of this doubleheader with a record of 70–61, five games behind the Boston Red Sox in the American League East. Jordan Montgomery takes the mound for New York in this second game of the doubleheader that will finish this three-game series. Montgomery owns a record of 7–6 and an ERA just above four. Francisco Lindor leads off the ball game with a single into right center field to Aaron Hicks, and Austin Jackson gets on base with a walk. The second baseman, José Ramírez, made a big impact in game one of the series with two solo homers, but he goes down swinging, and Montgomery gets his first strikeout. Edwin Encarnacion is batting with Lindor on second and Jackson on first with one out. Encarnacion sat out for the first game of this doubleheader as Yandy Díaz fills the role of designated hitter nicely with an RBI single in game one. Díaz is also playing in game two, as the designated hitter, Terry Francona, has Encarnacion playing first base. Two on one out and the 3–1 pitch to Encarnacion. He swings and lines an RBI single into centerfield; Lindor scores and Austin Jackson moves from first to third base on a throw that gets cut off by Greg Bird. It's now 1–0 Indians with runners at the corners with one out.

For the third straight game, the Indians have taken a first inning lead against New York. In recent ball games, the Indians have taken advantage of good scoring chances, and Carlos Santana comes to bat with that same opportunity and his team already in the lead. There's one out with runners at the comers for Santana; the 1–1 pitch, a swing, and line shot ricochets off the third base bag and carries into left field. Jackson scores to make it 2–0 on the RBI double by Santana, while Encarnacion stays at third. Manager Joe Girardi calls for an early time as he wants to try to calm his pitcher down. The Indians have two men in scoring position with one out, and the designated hitter Yandy Díaz is coming to bat. In game one of this doubleheader, Díaz was credited with the Indians-only RBI, as the first run was scored on a passed ball. Jordan Montgomery takes a deep breath, the 2–1 pitch, and Díaz swings and lines a single into left field. Edwin Encarnacion scores, and Carlos Santana slides in safely right behind him! It's a two-run single for Díaz and a four-run first for the Indians, and there is still only one out. Yandy Díaz, the Indians' reserve continues to shine.

On to the bottom of the first inning, Cleveland leads the Yankees as they erupted with four runs in the top half of the inning. The lefty Ryan Merritt takes the hill in this second game with a 1–0 record. Merritt made his last start on August 25 when he pitched six and two-thirds innings and helps lead the Indians to their league, leading thirteenth shutout of the season. Brett Gardner starts off the bottom of the inning with an infield single, and New York will try and cut into the Indians' lead. The second baseman, Starlin Castro, is up next, and the first pitch to Castro by Merritt and the ball is grounded to the Tribe's González, who throws to Ramírez at second who makes the turn and throws to Encarnacion as the Indians turn a five-four-three double play! Two quick outs for the Indians, and Gary Sánchez is the designated hitter for the Yankees in this second game. Joe Girardi probably wants to give him a break behind the plate, or one could argue that the Yankees want him to stop touching the baseball, as his play behind the plate has hurt them in this series. Sánchez takes the two-strike pitch and swings and loops a shallow fly ball caught by Jackson in center field for the third out. It's a strong start for Ryan Merritt as the Indians maintain their early 4–0 lead over the Yankees.

In Jordan Montgomery's second inning of work, he records a much-needed zero. The Indians don't score, and Edwin Encarnacion is stranded on first after reaching base with a two-out walk. The young slugger, Aaron Judge, leads off the bottom of the second with a ground ball that is mishandled by Lindor, and the partisans award

Judge with an infield hit. Judge is on first with nobody out as the shortstop, Didi Gregorius, steps up for his first at-bat of the game.

"Left on left, Merritt's pitch, Gregorius, lines it to left, but coming in and diving and making a great backhanded catch is Brandon Guyer! He rolls over throws into the infield, and Judge is back to first, and that is precluding big innings," announces Tom Hamilton.

Aaron Hicks gets aboard with a one-out single, and Aaron Judge advances to second. Greg Bird is the batter now with two men on base, and he is able cut into the four-run deficit with a single to Jackson in center field that scores Judge from second. The one-run spark by the Yankees is halted with a force-out hit by Ronald Torreyes, and the play is made by Erick González, who retires Greg Bird at second base. Austin Romine is out number 3 as he swings and hits a ground ball played again by the third baseman, González, who throws on to Encarnacion at first to end the inning. It is the last half of the fourth, and Aaron Judge leads off for New York, facing Ryan Merritt. Judge is 1–1 with a leadoff single, he came home to score on the RBI base hit by Greg Bird in the second inning. Merritt fires the 2–2 pitch, "and he's out looking. Ryan Merritt has his first strikeout tonight and sends Aaron Judge back to the dugout with the bat on his shoulder," Matt Underwood states. The shortstop, Didi Gregorius, steps up with the bases empty and one out. Gregorius is 0–1 with a line drive out that was made by the diving Brandon Guyer in left, preventing a big second inning. Ryan Merritt so far has pitched well; the Indians have a 4–1 lead, and for the most part, the Yankees haven't had many scoring chances. Gregorius awaits the 3–1 pitch, a swing, and a slow chopper to the mound as Merritt grabs the ball and throws on to first to retire Gregorius for the second out.

The Yankees get a two-out base runner with a single hit to Santana in right field by Aaron Hicks, but Greg Bird flies out to Austin Jackson in left to retire the side, and the Indians are coming to bat in the fifth. Austin Jackson took over the responsibility of playing in left field since Brandon Guyer left the game with injury after his diving grab in the bottom of the second inning. Bradley Zimmer is now playing in center field. The Yankees have made a pitching change to start the top of the fifth inning. Chasen Shreve replaces

Jordan Montgomery, who over four innings allows four-runs, all coming in the very first inning. First baseman, Edwin Encarnacion, leads off, and Shreve quickly has him down with two strikes.

The pitch, "Oh, Edwin just destroyed a ball to deep left field and gone! Maybe as high as it was far and that's home run number 31 for Edwin. Seventy-seventh run driven in, and it's now 5–1 Cleveland," Matt Underwood comments.

That leadoff home run adds to a three-run lead, a no-doubt-about-it blast to start the fifth. The Yankees do no damage in the bottom of the inning as the side is retired by Merritt. Ronald Torreyes grounds out to Lindor at short. The catcher, Austin Romine, hits a deep fly ball to right field but not deep enough as Carlos Santana makes the grab for out number 2. Ryan Merritt gets Starlin Castro to ground into a force out when Brett Gardner gets on base after an error by José Ramírez. The Yankees leave no men on base, and through five innings, Merritt has allowed just the one run. The Indians lead, 5–1, as we move to the top of the sixth. The Indians' Erik González starts off the inning facing Chasen Shreve, who took over the mound duties to begin the fifth. González is having a strong defensive game; he has been involved in several plays on the infield and has kept the Yankees from making noise with their bats. González is 0–1 with a line drive out and a walk, but he starts off the top of the sixth with a double on a ball that falls in front of Gardner in left.

With Gonzalez on second, Austin Jackson steps in now with one out as Lindor grounds out to Gregorius at short. Jackson is 1–2 and facing Shreve for the first time today. Chasen Shreve has Jackson down, 0–1, he checks second, the pitch, and Jackson swings and smokes a ball to deep center field, Hicks racing back as the ball hits off his glove and bangs up against the wall. González comes home to increase the lead to 6–1, and Jackson is 2–3 with a double and an RBI! The Yankees make another pitching change as Caleb Smith receives the bullpen call to replace Chasen Shreve with one out. Austin Jackson stays stranded as the top of the sixth ends with a strikeout, and Caleb Smith gets Encarnacion to chase a breaking ball for strike three. Encarnacion is now 2–3 with a single, a homer, and he has scored twice.

31

On to the bottom of the sixth, the designated hitter, Gary Sánchez, will lead off, and on the first pitch, he pops out to Erik González at third for the first out of the inning. Sánchez is now 0–3 on the day, and like most of his teammates, he is showing no production offensively. Aaron Judge is the second batter; he has scored the Yankees' only run and gets walked on nine pitches by Ryan Merritt with one out. Terry Francona makes the decision to turn to the bullpen, as Craig Breslow replaces Merritt, who goes five and one-third with one strikeout and one earned run given up. Breslow faces Didi Gregorius with Judge at first base and prepares to offer his 2–1 pitch. Gregorius hits a broken bat line drive toward the first base side, and Encarnacion grabs the ball with his glove and kicks the bag for an inning ending double play! It is an unassisted double play, as Edwin is quick with his feet and steps on the base before Judge could return safely! What a heads-up play by Encarnacion! The Indians pitching continues to roll, 6–1 Tribe, as we move to the seventh inning. Two out and one on for catcher Yan Gomes.

Prior to Gomes, Carlos Santana lines out to Aaron Judge in right, Bradley Zimmer lines out to Gardner in left, and Díaz is walked in between. Gomes is batting 0–3 today, and he has struck out in every at-bat. Gomes takes a first pitch strike from Caleb Smith. Now the one-strike pitch and Gomes swings and blasts a ball deep to right field down the line, inside the pole and gone! A two-run home run for Yan Gomes, his tenth, and it is an 8–1 Indians lead with two out in the seventh. We go to the top of the eighth, Cleveland still ahead of New York by seven in game 2 of this doubleheader, and the Yankees have made some defensive changes. Francisco Lindor is leading off for Cleveland; his only hit is a single that came in the top of the first inning. The Indians have hit the ball hard to every part of the field, and their pitching has been just as effective as the 8–1 lead demonstrates.

"Now the wind and the pitch to Lindor. It's swung on and hammered, high and deep to left field and gone! Frankie Lindor hits his twenty-fifth, ten of them right-handed. A moonshot in the Bronx, 9–1 Indians. What a day for Frankie Lindor!" Tom Hamilton comments.

Lindor's home run ties a franchise record for most home runs hit by an Indians' shortstop in a single season. He ties Asdrúbal Cabrera with home run number 25, and it is a memorable moment for the young man in just his third season with the Indians. In the bottom of the ninth, the Yankees cut into the eight-run lead with a three-run bomb hit by Greg Bird, but the Indians still lead, 9–4, with the Yankees down to their final out. Zach McAllister is now facing Austin Romine with two out and the bases empty.

"A swing and another pop-up, this again by the mound. This time the third baseman, Urshela, makes the catch…ball game! So the Cleveland Indians have swept the doubleheader from the Yankees. They have swept the three-game series, something they hadn't done in New York, a three-game sweep of a series since 1989," Tom Hamilton adds.

So the Tribe comes to New York and takes care of business with great hitting and pitching in all three games. It never hurts to get some help from your opponent, and the Indians take advantage of the Yankees' defensive struggles, scoring on wild pitches and a passed ball. But for most of this three-game series, the Tribe produces their own runs. The Yankees have always been a franchise that has been known to strike fear in their opponents, knowing almost any hitter can take you deep. In this series, however, it is the Indians who homer seven times, while the Yankees only hit the long ball twice. The Indians will travel to Detroit to meet their AL central rival for a four-game series that will start on September 1.

Chapter 3

※》》》 《《《※

No Slowing Down in Motown, Games 8–11

From Comerica Park in Detroit Michigan, it is game number 133. It is the Cleveland Indians and the Detroit Tigers. Tom Hamilton, along with Jim Rosenhaus, are once again announcing the game as the Indians come to Detroit to continue their eleven-game road trip. Comerica Park has been the Tigers' home since the year 2000, and it seats over 41,000 fans. The dimensions of this ballpark are 345 feet to left, 330 feet to right, and 420 feet to dead center.

On June 30, the Tigers and the Indians had a game postponed due to bad weather conditions, so these two ball clubs will play a four-game series rather than a three-game series and begin the doubleheader today. The Indians are coming off a three-game sweep in New York, winning the last game, 9-4, on August 30. In the previous series in New York, the Tribe also played in a doubleheader in games 2 and 3, so by the end of the day, the Indians will have played four games in three days. The Indians are 76–56 and stand in at first place in the Central Division, while the Tigers are 58–74, eighteen games in back of the Tribe. Matthew Boyd will be the starter for Detroit in game 1 of this doubleheader, and Francisco Lindor will lead off the game for the Indians. In Lindor's final at bat in game 3 against the Yankees, he hit his twenty-fifth home run that ties a franchise record for most home runs hit by an Indians' shortstop in a single season.

Francisco Lindor sits alongside former Indians shortstop, Asdrúbal Cabrera, who hit twenty-five home runs in 2011.

Matthew Boyd winds into his motion, and Lindor swings at the first pitch, and the ball is popped high in the air and caught by the first baseman, Efrén Navarro, for the first out. The Indians get a one out single from Austin Jackson, but José Ramírez chops the ball slowly to first and grounds into a three-six-three double play to end the top of the first inning. It is a good first inning defensively by the Tigers' first baseman, Navarro, who participates in all three outs to set down the Indians. Carlos Carrasco is the Tribe's starting pitcher in the first game of today's doubleheader. Carrasco is searching for win number 14. He dominated the Kansas City Royals lineup, pitching seven scoreless innings in the Indians' 12–0 victory five days ago. The first batter today facing Carlos Carrasco is the Tigers' second baseman, Ian Kinsler. Carrasco offers his one-strike pitch, and Kinsler swings and hits a ground ball fielded by Giovanny Urshela at third, who throws to Encarnacion for out number 1. The last time these division rivals met, it was the final game before the All-Star Break when the Tigers overcame the Indians by a score of 5–3 on July 9 in Cleveland. Alex Presley steps in; he is playing in right field in game 1 of this doubleheader. Carrasco sends his pitch, and that ball is grounded softly to José Ramírez, who throws to first in time for the second out.

Miguel Cabrera is batting third and is the designated hitter for Detroit. The first two batters are retired very quickly by Carrasco, so Cabrera will try to extend this first inning for the Tigers. Carrasco's 2–2 pitch and Cabrera sendds a high fly ball to center field, but Austin Jackson makes the grab, and the Tigers go one, two, three. We move ahead to the bottom of the second, the Indians are kept off the scoreboard in the top half in which they leave two base runners stranded as Yan Gomes grounded out to Matthew Boyd for the third out. In the bottom of the second, Nick Castellanos lines out to the Tribe's center fielder, Austin Jackson, who doesn't even need to move to make the catch. Mikie Mahtook steps in for his first at-bat of the ball game. Mahtook awaits the 1–0 pitch by Carrasco...and Mahtook just got hit by the pitch. So the Tigers get a one out base runner for Efrén Navarro. One out and a man on first base after Mahtook stays in the game.

Carrasco checks the sign from Gomes; here is the pitch, and it is swung on, and the ball is grounded to short and played by Francisco Lindor, who retires Navarro at first. Mahtook advances to second, but there are two out. The catcher, James McCann, is batting with the go-ahead run standing on second base, but the Tigers have two outs. McCann is down, 1–2, the pitch by Carrasco and strike 3 called! A fastball on the outer half of the plate as Carrasco gets his first strike-out, and the Tigers leave a man stranded in scoring position. The Tigers and the Indians have played two scoreless innings, and in the top of the third inning, Matthew Boyd retires the Indians in order. Frankie Lindor and Austin Jackson both go down on strikeouts, giving Boyd three punch-outs already in the game. In the bottom of the third inning, the Tigers' center fielder, JaCoby Jones, is the leadoff man for Detroit. Jones is down in the count with a ball and two strikes; he is battling hard, fouling off Carrasco's last three pitches. Carrasco takes the sign from his catcher…the pitch is swung on and missed! It got him swinging on- an off-speed pitch for the first out.

José Iglesias hits a one-out single to Brandon Guyer in left, and the Tigers get their first base hit. Ian Kinsler steps up for his second at-bat; he is 0–1 with a groundout to Giovanny Urshela. Kinsler swings at the first pitch; the ball is swung on and grounded to Lindor, who throws Iglesias out at second. Ramírez makes the turn for an inning ending six-four-three double play. Carlos Carrasco looks sharp after three innings, only allowing the one hit, and he has struck out two batters. As we move along to the top of the fifth, we are still scoreless after four innings in Detroit. Brandon Guyer is batting with one out after Yandy Díaz grounded out on a ball that hit Boyd in the leg, and third baseman Nick Castellanos makes an outstanding barehanded grab to throw Díaz out at first base. Guyer swings at the 2–0 pitch; that ball is played by Kinsler, and Guyer is out. The play is reviewed and overturned, as Efrén Navarro never keeps his foot on first base, and Guyer is ruled safe. So the Indians have a base runner.

Yan Gomes steps in with a one-out base runner, the pitch to him, and he takes high for ball 1. It seems like Boyd is having issue with his command ever since that line drive hit him in the leg. When he made his delivery, his back foot is slipping. The next pitch and Gomes swings and grounds a single into right field for a base hit, and Guyer advances to second. Gio Urshela is batting, and the Indians have Gomes on first, Guyer on second and just one out. Matthew Boyd makes his first pitch, and Urshela swings and lines a single into right field; Guyer is waved home, and the Indians grab a 1–0 lead. Gomes moves to third, and the Tribe has the lead with runners at the corners with only one out. Francisco Lindor is batting with a 1–0 lead from the RBI single by Urshela. Lindor is 0–1 after he popped out to first baseman, Efrén Navarro, in the top of the first. Now he will look to drive home more runs for his team. The 3–0 pitch and ball 4, and as Lindor takes his base, Gio Urshela moves to second, and the bases are loaded for the Indians.

The Indians lead, 1–0, and Jackson steps in; he is 1–2 with a single and a strikeout. Matthew Boyd makes his seventh pitch and swing, and a miss, Jackson is out, number 2 striking out for a second time. The side is retired as José Ramírez swings and flies out to Alex Presley in right field, and the Indians leave them loaded and only plate one run. That is uncommon for Ramírez, as he has recently found ways to be a prolific run producer for the Indians. The Tigers are batting in the fifth down a run, and Mikie Mahtook will bat first. Mahtook got hit by a pitch in the second inning but was stranded on base after Carrasco struck out James McCann for the third out. Mahtook is batting with two strikes, the 1–2 pitch, a swing and a miss! A breaking ball that Mahtook swings over the top of, he is a little too aggressive. Navarro is batting with one out; he is 0–1, facing Carrasco with a groundout to short in the second inning. Carrasco has Navarro down, 1–2, the pitch, a swing, and a miss, and Carrasco has five strikeouts and two quick outs in the inning. Back-to-back strikeouts on Mahtook and Navarro and James McCann will bat with the bases empty. The first pitch by Carrasco and McCann swings and lines a ball to José Ramírez at second, who can't come up with the ball cleanly; the play is ruled an infield hit, and Detroit gets an extra out to work with.

The center fielder, JaCoby Jones, continues the inning with a two out single to Guyer in left, and the Tigers have the tying and go-ahead runs on base with José Iglesias stepping up to the plate. Iglesias is batting with an even count, the pitch, and that ball is swung on and lined into the left center field gap, and McCann scores to tie the game at one. So the Tigers get some two out magic brewing and tie this game. The RBI single by José Iglesias also gets JaCoby Jones to third, and before Ian Kinsler would bat, we have a mound visit. Carlos Carrasco and the Indians avoid any more damage, as Kinsler is the third out grounding out softly to Francisco Lindor. Detroit leaves the go-ahead run stranded at third, and the game is even at one as we begin the top half of the sixth. The Detroit Tigers have made a pitching change to start the sixth inning and replaced Matthew Boyd with Drew VerHagen. First baseman Edwin Encarnacion will lead off the sixth inning for Cleveland in this tie ball game. This is the first batter for VerHagen, and here is the 1–0 pitch. It is swung on blasted by Encarnacion to deep left field, and that ball is gone! Home run number 32 for Encarnacion as it goes beyond the Tiger bullpen, and the Indians waste no time regaining the lead; it is now 2–1 on the leadoff solo home run by Encarnacion. Just two pitches to retake the lead, and Encarnacion tallies his seventy-ninth RBI!

In the bottom of the sixth inning, Nick Castellanos is batting with two down after Presley and Cabrera are set down on a pop-out and a line out. The pitch, the swing, and Castellanos gets a two-out single on a sharp ground ball hit to Jackson in center field. That ball kicks off the foot of José Ramírez and makes its way to center for a hit. Mikie Mahtook will bat with the tying run on base, but Carrasco has Mahtook down, 1–2. Carrasco checks the runner, the pitch, and the swing and a miss by Mahtook! Strikeout number 6 for Carrasco, and the Indians maintain their one-run lead; it is 2–1 Indians moving to the bottom of the eighth inning. Calling for a pitching change for the Indians, Terry Francona summons Bryan Shaw to take over for Carlos Carrasco, who pitches seven innings and records eight strikeouts. He is in position to win this ball game if the bull pen can close it out. Bryan Shaw is facing Ian Kinsler, who is hitless in three at-bats. Shaw has Kinsler down, 1–2, the pitch, and he swings as he leans away, but his bat gets a piece of the ball, and Gomes hangs on for the strikeout. It isn't much of an attempt, but the Tigers have one out in the eighth with Alex Presley batting next.

The one-strike pitch by Shaw and Presley gets on base with a one-out line-drive single into right field. Two outs now after Miguel Cabrera is Shaw's second strikeout victim of the inning, Cabrera chases ball 4 in the dirt. Nick Castellanos is batting with Presley on first; the score is 2–1 Indians. Castellanos is 1–3, reaching base with a single in the sixth inning. Bryan Shaw makes his pitch, and Castellanos lines a single into right field. Presley holds at third, and the tying run is ninety feet away for Mikie Mahtook. Cleveland makes another pitching change—closer Cody Allen replaces Bryan Shaw. Allen has Mahtook down, 1–2, as he delivers the pitch, a swing, and a slow chopper to Lindor, who bobbles the baseball; everybody is safe. Presley scores, and we are tied at two. Efrén Navarro is retired on a fly ball to Zimmer in center field, who replaced Austin Jackson, but the Tigers retie the game in the eighth on a two-out infield hit by Mikie Mahtook.

The Tigers call on pitcher Shane Greene to begin the ninth inning in this 2–2 ball game. Abraham Almonte will pinch-hit for Yan Gomes. Almonte lines out to José Iglesias for the first out of the ninth inning. Jay Bruce will also bat as a pinch-hitter for Giovanny Urshela as the Indians look to find a way to take back the lead before the bottom of the ninth inning. Shane Greene offers his 1–2 pitch, and Bruce swings and hits a long fly ball carrying deep; the ball hits against the wall in right center, and Bruce makes the turn for third and bags a triple! It is the first triple of the season for Jay Bruce, and the Indians quickly get the go-ahead run in scoring position with one out and Lindor batting next. Francisco Lindor wants to make up for his mistake in the eighth inning that allowed the Tigers to tie this game; Jay Bruce is standing on third with one out.

"It's a 2–2 tie, infield in, the pitch, Lindor with a line-drive base hit center field! He nearly decapitated Shane Greene. The Indians take a 3–2 lead, and Frankie Lindor blisters a single to center to drive in Jay Bruce," Tom Hamilton announces.

We go to the bottom of the ninth inning—Cleveland 3, Detroit 2. Cody Allen stays in for the Indians; he will try and finish off the Tigers with his club, leading by a run. The 0–1 pitch to James McCann, and he swings and hits a leadoff single to right field. The Tigers now have the winning run at the plate. JaCoby Jones is out number 1 as he swings and misses on a good breaking ball by Cody Allen. The Tigers call for a pinch runner; Andrew Romine will run for James McCann at first base with one out. Two outs now and the bases are loaded after two, two out singles by José Iglesias and Alex Presley. The Indians are clinging to a 3–2 lead, and the fans at Comerica park are making some noise, as they want to see a walk-off win for their Tigers. Terry Francona replaces Cody Allen for the side-winder, Joe Smith. The Indians acquired Smith from the Blue Jays at the trade deadline. For Joe Smith, this is a familiar team, as he was with the Indians from 2009 to 2013. The Tigers are down a run with the bases loaded and two out. One ball one strike on Miguel Cabrera.

"They're enjoying this possibility of an upset. The pitch, swung on lined to short caught by Lindor, ball game! Well, Cabrera can't hit it any harder. If it's not at Lindor, the Tigers win. But the Indians survive in game 1 on a base loaded bullet out to the shortstop Frankie Lindor, who in essence won the game for the Indians with a ninth inning RBI single after the pinch-hit triple by Jay Bruce," comments Tom Hamilton.

Joe Smith gets his first save since returning to the Indians; Cody Allen gets the win, and the Indians take game one against the Tigers by a final score of 3–2.

From the Motor City in Detroit, Michigan, it is the Detroit Tigers and the Cleveland Indians, as both clubs are just about ready for game two of this day/night doubleheader, part of this four-game series. The Indians took game one of the doubleheader earlier in the day by a score of 3–2. The Tigers had the bases loaded with Miguel Cabrera batting, facing Joe smith in the ninth inning, and the Indians escaped with a win as Cabrera lined out to Lindor to end game one. The Indians have the opportunity to sweep back to back doubleheaders on the road with a win tonight. They are in first place in the Central Division with a record of 77–56. The Indians are also playing for a second nine-game winning streak of the season, which would tie the longest win streak for the Indians of this 2017 campaign. From July 21 to 29, the Indians swept the Toronto Blue Jays in a three-game series. They won the makeup game, 6–2, against the Cincinnati Reds on July 24. Then the Los Angeles Angels got swept by the Tribe in three games, and they went on to beat the Chicago White Sox in two of the first three ball games on the road. Buck Farmer will be on the mound for the Tigers in our second game; Bradley Zimmer will hit first for the Indians. Zimmer is not normally the leadoff batter for the Indians, but it seems Lindor has been given this game off.

The pitch, Zimmer on strike 1 swings and grounds out to Miguel Cabrera playing first base for out number 1. Yandy Díaz is batting second, and he is quickly down, 0–2. The pitch and strike 3 called! So it is Buck Farmer with strikeout number one and two fast outs to start the first inning. The Indians go quietly as Jay Bruce flies out to JaCoby Jones in shallow center field, and the Tigers will bat in the bottom half of the inning to see what they can do facing Mike Clevinger. Ian Kinsler is the leadoff man in this scoreless game in the bottom of the first inning facing Mike Clevinger. The Tribe's starter is pitching with an extra day off since the Wahoos did not play on the thirty-first. Clevinger's last appearance was on August 26 when he pitched six innings against the Kansas City Royals and earned his seventh win in the Tribe's 4–0 victory. Kinsler swings at the first pitch and skies the ball to the first base side, and Santana makes the easy grab in foul territory for the out.

Alex Presley is now batting with one out as Kinsler is set down on the first pitch. Clevinger has Presley down, 1–2, the pitch, and it's a called strike 3! Presley just lets that fastball go right over the plate; there are two outs now as Clevinger has his first strikeout, two batters in! Miguel Cabrera, batting third in today's game, had the opportunity to be the hero in game one but was denied the game winning single by Francisco Lindor with the bases loaded in the ninth inning. The pitch and another pop-up to Carlos Santana, he makes the grab again in foul territory, and the first inning is over. Like the Indians, the Tigers have a slow start, going three up, three down. We head to the top of the second inning, Cleveland, 0, and Detroit, 0.

Edwin Encarnacion is batting cleanup for the Indians, and Terry Francona has him back as the designated hitter. Encarnacion is having a good at-bat, taking three close throws that are just off the plate. The 3–0 pitch is low ball 4, and Buck Farmer walks the leadoff batter to start the inning. In the past few games, Encarnacion has been reaching base with consistency, driving in runs, hitting the ball over the fence, and, in this case, taking the free pass. Carlos Santana is batting with a man on and nobody out. Farmer makes his pitch, and Santana pops the ball very high on the infield for out number one as the shortstop, Dixon Machado, makes the grab. Giovanny Urshela is batting now with two gone and two on with Encarnacion on second as he moves up after Chisenhall was hit by the pitch in the arm. Buck Farmer sends his payoff pitch, and Gio Urshela swings and lines the ball into the right field gap; the ball drops beyond Alex Presley, and coming home are Encarnacion and Chisenhall on the two-out, two-run double by Urshela!

We move to the bottom of the second now as the Tigers trail the Indians by a pair of runs. Nick Castellanos is facing Mike Clevinger, who has him down, 1–2. The pitch and strike 3 called on a fastball on the outer half of home plate. Two outs now as Mikie Mahtook flies out to Bradley Zimmer. But the Tigers have a chance for some two-out noise as Clevinger surrenders his first walk to John Hicks on nine pitches. With the first at-bat for the shortstop, Dixon Machado, Clevinger is trying to make a good pitch as he has Machado in an even 2–2 count. He agrees with his catcher, the pitch, and it is a swing and a miss! Clevinger buries his breaking ball in the dirt and got Machado to chase for his third strikeout. Buck Farmer and the Tigers have a quick third inning defensively; three up and three down go the Indians. Farmer gets his third strikeout, getting the leadoff man, Bradley Zimmer, who is caught looking at a fastball. The score is 2–0 Indians as Mike Clevinger goes back to the mound; it is now the bottom of the third inning. Like Buck Farmer, Clevinger has three strikeouts on the day so far. Andrew Romine, the leadoff batter, takes a hack and sends a leadoff double to Jay Bruce to begin the bottom of the third inning. Romine is the first base runner to be in scoring position for the Tigers.

For the first time today, Clevinger is pitching with a minor mess; JaCoby Jones is batting for the first time with a chance to cut the Indians' lead in half or perhaps tie the game. Clevinger today has been working ahead of batters but is now behind Jones, 3–0. Jones swings and hits a sharp line drive to left field right into Lonnie Chisenhall's glove for the first out. Ian Kinsler steps up for his second at-bat; he is 0–1 with a pop-out to Carlos Santana in the first inning. Kinsler in this at bat is battling hard as he works the count full.

"Kinsler grounds one towards the hole at short, backhanded by Urshela, off-balance long throw got him at first! What a play by a third baseman playing short!" Tom Hamilton exclaims.

Andrew Romine has made it to third base with two down, and Presley will bat next. The score remains 2–0 Indians, and it is Clevinger with two strikes on Presley and Romine at third as Mike Clevinger is trying to keep it that way. The pitch to Presley is swung on and missed! That is the fourth strikeout now for Clevinger, as he escapes the small jam, forcing the Tigers to leave a runner stranded at third base. That is the second time Presley has been struck out; he was caught looking the first time.

As we go to the top of the fourth inning, it is the Tribe leading the Tigers, 2–0. Edwin Encarnacion gets walked again by Buck Farmer; that is the second at-bat in a row Encarnacion gets walked to lead off an inning. He is one of two base runners that came home in the second inning on the double by Urshela. Carlos Santana is now batting, and he is 0–1, previously popping out to shortstop Dixon Machado. Farmer offers his first pitch, and Santana lines a base hit to Alex Presley in right field. Edwin Encarnacion is now on second with no outs, and Lonnie Chisenhall bats with two men on. Buck Farmer is having a difficult time finding the zone against Chisenhall; it is a 3–1 count, and if he is not careful with his next pitch, it could lead to trouble. Two on and nobody out, the 3–1 pitch to Chisenhall and its high, ball 4. So for the third time today, the Indians reach base with a walk, and this time, the bases are loaded with zero out and nowhere to put Roberto Pérez. It is the top of the fourth, 2–0 Indians, and they are looking to score more runs. Farmer has a full count on Pérez, the pitch swing and a fly ball to center falling in for a hit. Encarnacion scores, Carlos Santana is right behind him, and the Indians take a 4–0 lead on the two-run single by Roberto Pérez, and still nobody is out.

The Tigers call for a pitching change, and the lefty Blaine Hardy will take over. Buck Farmer leaves the game but could be charged with a fifth run if Chisenhall comes home to score. Giovanny Urshela is facing Hardy for the first time in the game. Urshela has two RBIs on the double he hit to right field in the second inning. Hardy is ahead of Urshela, 0-1, the pitch, and Urshela swings and delivers a ground ball played by Andrew Romine, who turns two; it is a four-six-three twin killer, and Lonnie Chisenhall is now standing at third. Erik González is now batting with two outs and stands in at 0–1 in this game. Blaine Hardy winds up to deliver the pitch to González with a 1–1 count, trying to avoid more damage. Hardy's pitch is swung on, and a blooper falls just in front of Mahtook; Chisenhall scores easily, and it is 5–0 Indians in the fourth inning.

In the top of the fourth, the Indians added three runs to their lead, and Clevinger continues to pitch well as he sets down Miguel Cabrera for out number one. The tally is 5–0 Tribe, and Nick Castellanos heads to the plate; he is 0–1 for the day, striking out in the second inning. Mike Clevinger works with a 0–2 count and sends the pitch, and the Tigers' right fielder swings and loops a pop-up to the Indians' second baseman, González; that is two quick outs for Clevinger and the Indians. The Tigers have not had much luck so far today, just one hit, and they have stranded two men on base as Clevinger has been superb. With two outs in the bottom of the fourth for the Tigers, the score remains 5–0 Indians. Mikie Mahtook bats with the bases empty; he is 0–1 on the day with a fly out to Bradley Zimmer. Mike Clevinger slings his sixth pitch to Mahtook with the count 2–2. He is into the motion, the pitch, and the home plate arbitrator calls strike three on the inner half of the plate! That is strikeout number five for Clevinger as we move ahead to the top of the sixth inning at Comerica Park in the Motor City; Cleveland leads Detroit by five runs.

Blaine Hardy is still pitching as he was summoned to replace Buck Farmer in the fourth. Roberto Pérez is leading off; he is 1–2 with a two-run single in the fourth inning off Farmer. Detroit's hurler tosses his first pitch, and it is belted as Pérez drives the ball deep to left field over the wall beyond the Tiger bullpen for a lead-off home run! It is 6–0 Indians in the sixth, Roberto Pérez with his fourth homer of the season and his third RBI in this game. Giovanny Urshela bats second in the inning; he is 1–2, driving in two runs. Hardy quickly strikes out Urshela on three pitches for out number one, and he notches his first strikeout. The Tigers are already down by six runs, and if they are going to push for a comeback, they can't allow any more runs to cross home plate. Erik González is now at-bat for a third time today; he has an RBI single that scored Chisenhall earlier in the contest. Hardy makes his pitch, and González smokes a one-out single into right for his second hit tonight. Bradley Zimmer is now the batter for the Tribe with one out, and González is the runner at first base. Zimmer is hitless so far this evening, 0–3, as he lined out his last at-bat. Zimmer has the count in his favor at 1–0… the pitch, Zimmer's swing, and the ball is smoked into right field. González goes all the way to third, and Bradley Zimmer gets a one-out double on what is normally a routine single, but he has the speed to take chances, and he slides into second safely!

Yandy Díaz will bat with two runners in scoring position and the Tribe already leading by half a dozen runs. Before Díaz takes his swings, the Detroit Tigers will make a second pitching change. Jeff Ferrell is the new pitcher with one out with second and third base occupied. Díaz is 0–2 today, and in this at-bat, he is batting with a 2–2 count. Ferrell makes the pitch, and the Tribe's versatile utility player swings and loops a base hit to center field. Two singles and a double increase this already big lead, and the Indians want to keep the line moving. González comes home on the RBI single, Zimmer moves to third, and the Indians tack on one more to lead by seven. Yandy Díaz is the runner now on first base; he has a five-game hit streak! Jay Bruce is the batter, and there is still only one out as the

Indians have three straight hits after the Urshela strikeout. Jay Bruce is 0–3 today with two fly outs and a pop out in the top of the fifth inning. The count moves to 1–1, and the pitch to Bruce is lofted to left center. JaCoby Jones runs down the ball for the out, but a sacrifice fly scores Zimmer from third and makes it 8–0 Cleveland.

It is a rough night for Detroit as they keep falling further behind. They were already down by five to start this inning, but hit or no hit, the Indians have added on three more runs in this sixth inning. There are two outs now after the sacrifice fly by Bruce that put the Indians up 8–0, and Edwin Encarnacion now bats with a runner on first. Encarnacion is 1–1 for the contest; this is his fourth at-bat, and he has walked twice.

"The payoff pitch swung on ripped up the ally in left center. It's a gapper that will score Díaz…it will roll to the wall. Encarnacion is on his way to second with an RBI, 9–0 Indians," Tom Hamilton announces.

Carlos Santana steps to the dish as the Indians' bats continue to make a statement, scoring four times in this sixth inning. The pitch to Santana, a swing, and Carlos Santana lines an RBI single to center field! Encarnacion comes home from second, and the Indians with their sixth hit of the inning now lead the Tigers by ten runs as Carlos Santana gets his seventy-first RBI. The Tigers finally retire the side but not before the Indians score five more runs to double their lead; it is now 10–0! We move to the bottom of the ninth inning now, and the Tribe's Nick Goody is pitching, and this game is all but over already. The Indians have scored ten times and have a 10–0 lead with two down and Dixon Machado the batter.

"The pitch swung on lined to center, and Zimmer is there to make the catch, ball game! And a major league leading sixteen shutouts for the Tribe, and they have their second nine-game win streak of the year. They bury the Tigers in the night cap by a final score of ten to nothing!" Tom Hamilton comments.

Mike Clevinger is the winning pitcher for the Indians, and he is outstanding with six strikeouts and the shutout. The Indians have now swept both road doubleheaders against the New York Yankees and now the Detroit Tigers. The Indians record win number 78, and for the first time since 1954, this franchise has won nine straight games twice in the same season.

It is the third game of this four-game series between the Tigers and the Indians as Cleveland plays their sixth straight road game. The Indians start this game with a record of 78–56; they are in first place in the Central Division and have tied a season best nine-game win streak with yesterday's 10–0 blowout victory. The Tigers are 58–76, fourth place in the division, twenty games behind these red-hot Indians. The Tigers will start the righty Jordan Zimmerman; he is 8–11 this year and really having a tough time with an ERA above six. Frankie Lindor is the leadoff slugger as he steps to the plate, anxious to get underway. Lindor had the previous game off as he watched his teammates cruise to their sixteenth shutout of the year and their ninth straight win! Zimmerman makes the first pitch as the man behind the dish calls strike 1, and we are underway in Detroit. Zimmerman tosses his next pitch, and Lindor smokes a ball to deep right, but racing to the track is Alex Presley for the first out. Center fielder Bradley Zimmer bats second today for the Indians. The 1–0 pitch is delivered, and Zimmer responds with a deep drive to right; it is a long run for the Tigers' fielders, and the ball drops in between Presley and Mahtook as Zimmer rounds second base easily and races to third with a one-out triple.

Two batters into the game and the Indians have the go-ahead run at third base, and José Ramírez, the league leader in doubles, is the batter. Ramírez fights hard to bring home Zimmer from third base, battling with a 3–2 count.

Zimmerman's "Payoff pitch, swung on, this is hit very deep to left center field. Mahtook, racing back, can't make the catch. Ball hits the track and bangs up against the wall. Ramírez around second, he's on his way to third in sliding, back to back triples! In to score is Zimmer," Tom Hamilton says.

So it is a quick first inning run scored by the Indians and Ramírez with his sixth triple of the season. Now batting with a 1–0 lead is the Tribe's designated hitter, Edwin Encarnacion. Ramírez camps on third with one out, and Encarnacion bats with the Tiger infield moved in. Zimmerman falls behind 3–0 to Encarnacion, and the Tigers' hurler will need to be careful where he places this next pitch. Here it comes, a swing and a base hit into center field for Encarnacion. José Ramírez can jog home, and it is 2–0 Indians with one out in the first inning. A grounder up the middle for Edwin, he doesn't hit the ball hard but doesn't need to. Carlos Santana is the batter, and Zimmerman has Santana down with two strikes, looking for a much-needed strikeout. Zimmerman with the 1–2 pitch, Santana swings and hits a deep drive to right center field, and this ball hits the wall. Encarnacion saunters all the way to third base on the stand-up double by Santana, and there are two on now and only one out.

The Indians are already in front with a four hit, two-run inning, giving Zimmerman all he can handle as Chisenhall bats with one out and two men in scoring position. Chisenhall offers at the first pitch, and the ball is popped high on the infield to third, and Jeimer Candelario makes the grab in foul ground for the second out. Now batting for the Indians is the left fielder, Abraham Almonte. It is 2–0 Indians with runners on second and third base for Almonte, who is trying to do more first inning damage.

On the first pitch, "He bangs one back up the middle and into center field! That will score Encarnacion and Santana. It's a four-run first, Abe Almonte!" Tom Hamilton exclaims.

Yan Gomes bags a two-out single, moving Almonte to third base, but the Tigers get Gio Urshela to line out to Andrew Romine in left for the third out, and it is a 4–0 Tribe lead after half of an inning. The Indians' ace, Corey Kluber, gets the start in game three, and when Kluber is given four runs early, you could pretty much hit the showers if you are the opposition. Corey Kluber with a record of 13–4 this season and an ERA below three, as he is in the running to be honored with his second Cy Young award at the end of this season. The Tigers' second baseman, Ian Kinsler, is in the leadoff spot with his team trailing the Indians, 4–0. Kluber sets, the first pitch is swung on and grounded to Lindor, who makes the throw to get Kinsler at first base. A quick out for Kluber but on a 1–1 pitch, Alex Presley swings and hits a single that falls in front of Bradley Zimmer in center, and the Tigers will try and make up some ground with the one out single. Nick Castellanos, the designated hitter, faces Corey Kluber with Presley on base; he is trying to find a gap in the outfield to move up or score the runner. Kluber with the first offering, a swing by Castellanos is grounded to Lindor, who throws to Ramírez at second to retire Presley, and Ramírez makes the turn to record the inning ending double play! No strikeouts for Kluber, but he sets down the Tigers with less than ten pitches, and the Tigers are behind, 4–0, after the first inning.

It is the bottom of the second inning now with a score of 4–0 Indians as Jordan Zimmerman puts up a zero in the top half while keeping two Tribe runners on base. Corey Kluber hustles back to the mound to face Efrén Navarro. Navarro with an even 1–1 count fouls off the tough breaking ball to fall behind in the count, 1–2. Kluber's next pitch is swung on and missed! Navarro chases the fastball high and out of the strike zone for out number one and strikeout number one. Mikie Mahtook is the fifth batter for the Tigers in the lineup as the Motown Mob is down by four just trying to get a rally going. The first pitch by Kluber is low, ball one. Kluber works quickly, making the pitch, a swing, but Mahtook holds up for ball two with no strikes. The count moves to an even 2–2 with the pitch by Kluber, a swing by Mahtook, and the ball is chopped fair to Gio at third base. Urshela, with a backhanded grab and throw, gets Mikie Mahtook on a nice grab by Santana at first to get the second out! This Indians defense in the last nine games has just been sensational, as they seem to make a highlight reel play every game. Two outs now and the bases empty for Jeimer Candelario, the third baseman is longing for his first at-bat today against Kluber. With a one-ball, two-strike count, the pitch is swung on and missed!

Candelario is Kluber's second strikeout victim as he chases the inside off-speed toss for the third out of the frame. It is the bottom of the third inning now, and catcher Bryan Holaday swings and hits a gapper toward Zimmer in center who is on the run and dives for the ball, but it ricochets off his glove for a leadoff double. Bradley Zimmer bangs his head on the grass diving for the ball and leaves the game to get checked out. The rookie, Greg Allen, comes in to take over in center field for the Tribe. Bryan Holaday is on third now with two out as Ian Kinsler tries to get a big hit to trim the Cleveland lead to three or less. Kinsler is 0–1 so far with a groundout. Kluber works to a full count on Kinsler and makes the payoff pitch, a swing, and a blooper right at Santana, who makes the grab to retire Kinsler and the Tigers. As we move to the bottom of the fourth, the Indians' bats have gone silent since the first inning. Jordan Zimmerman has regained his command since the four run first inning; although he has given up four hits, he has stranded all four runners and notched two strikeouts. There is one out now as Nick Castellanos smokes the ball into Urshelas's glove at third after a lead off-base hit by Presley into left field.

Mikie Mahtook bats now with runners on first and third after a single by Efrén Navarro. With one out, the Tigers bat in this fourth inning down by four runs and so far have had a rough day facing Corey Kluber. Detroit has only struck out twice in three and one-third innings, but that doesn't matter as long as you find a way to keep the opposition from crossing home plate, and Kluber has. The 0–2 pitch is delivered to Mahtook, who swings and misses at the breaking pitch, moving down and away into the opposite batter's box. Kluber records his third strikeout as he makes Mahtook look silly swinging at that offering. Now with two on, two out, Jeimer Candelario tries to find a way to bring home some runs. The Tigers' third baseman works to a full count with Candelario fouling away three pitches in this at-bat. The pitch, a swing, and a ground ball to Santana who makes an easy play as he steps on the bag, and the inning is over. We've played four innings in Detroit—Cleveland, 4, and Detroit, 0. Carlos Santana leads off the top of the fifth inning; he is 1–2 with a double and a run scored in the first inning.

Jordan Zimmerman's pitching is much improved since the first inning, but four runs could be enough when your batters are facing one of the top pitchers in the American League. Carlos Santana swings and hits a deep drive into left but directly at Andrew Romine as the first out is made. Lonnie Chisenhall, now batting, is hitless facing Zimmerman in two at-bats. Chisenhall takes ball one from Zimmerman, showing good patience and waiting for a better pitch to hit. The 1–0 pitch, a swing, and Lonnie smokes this ball over the head of Navarro and into the right field corner for a one-out double! Left fielder Abraham Almonte steps into the box next; he is 1–2 with two runs driven in today. Chisenhall stands on second after the double he launches to the corner in right and a four-run lead. Almonte takes ball one from Zimmerman for a 1–0 count. The pitch, a swing, and Almonte lines this ball over the head of the short-stop, José Iglesias. Chisenhall is waved home, and now the throw to second and in sliding safely is Abe Almonte, who has two hits and three RBIs! At 5–0, the Indians lead the Tigers, scoring for the first time since the four-run first inning.

The Indians' hitting and pitching are in complete control of this game, moving now to the bottom of the ninth inning. With a 5–1 Indians lead, we move to the final frame for the Tigers, who scored their only run on a single by Bryan Holaday against Kluber in the seventh inning. Mikie Mahtook is on third base, Candelario on first with two outs, and José Iglesias is batting; he is 0–3, striking out twice against Kluber. Cody Allen has just come in to replace Bryan Shaw, who has been unable to get the final out. The pitch, a swing, and a base hit into right field, and Mahtook scores to make it 5–2 Indians; with two outs, the Tigers are showing signs of life. It is now a save situation for Allen as the second baseman, Ian Kinsler, will bat as the potential tying run. The Tribe closer works to a full count on Kinsler, the pitch by Cody Allen.

"Swung on soft one hopper to short, Lindor gloves, throws, ball game! So it got dicey in the ninth inning, but Cody Allen able to rack up save number twenty-three, and the Indians have a season best ten-game win streak! They stop the Detroit Tigers tonight by a final score of 5–2," announces Tom Hamilton.

During the postgame, manager Terry Francona raves about the great game pitched by Corey Kluber and how he made the runs hold up. Francona, in referring to the four-run first inning, said, "We didn't do a lot after that, but it's a good way to play, especially when Kluber's pitching." Francona also spoke about giving players like Greg Allen experience and how it is nice to play anybody on the roster and still be able to win games.

It is the first week of September and the final game at Comerica Park between the Detroit Tigers and the Cleveland Indians. The Indians are in position to sweep their third straight series, which would give them their eleventh straight win! After this game, the Indians travel to Chicago to play four more road games against the White Sox before they finally come home from this long road trip. Chad Bell starts the final game of this four-game series for the Tigers; he is 0–1 with an ERA above five. The Wahoo's José Ramírez bats with two outs as Francisco Lindor grounds out to Kinsler at second and Austin Jackson strikes out swinging on six pitches. Bell falls behind Ramírez, pitching now with a 3–1 count.

"The pitch swung on this is ripped to deep left field…this ball is gone! Or is it? It is gone! It hit the top of the fence and ricocheted in the air and kind of a second look by third base ump, Ryan Blakney, and he finally said, 'That's a home run.' A bullet to left off the bat of José Ramírez," Tom Hamilton says.

Very strange how that played out as Mikie Mahtook, when the ball bounces off the wall, tries to play it with his bare hand and knocks it over the wall for a home run. So fourteen pitches made by Chad Bell, and it is a 1–0 lead for the Tribe on a solo homer by Ramírez, his twenty-first of the year. The designated hitter, Edwin Encarnacion, bats fourth; he swings at the first pitch and flies out to JaCoby Jones in center field to end the inning, but the Indians do take a one-run lead to start the game as we move on to the Tiger half of the first. Josh Tomlin is the Tribe's starter; he is 7–9 with an ERA above five. This is Tomlin's first game back from the disabled list since July 30 in Chicago. Francona said before the game they didn't want to make Tomlin work more than he needed to.

Ian Kinsler bats for Detroit, already finding himself and his teammates behind in this game after half of an inning. Roberto Pérez is playing catcher for Josh Tomlin, who fires strike 1 past Kinsler. Ian Kinsler takes the next pitch low to even the count. The 1–1 pitch by Tomlin and Kinsler swings and hits this ball that will fall in front of Guyer in right field for a leadoff single. Alex Presley bats next as the potential go-ahead run. Presley works to a full count as Tomlin's last four pitches have been fouled out of play, making this next pitch the tenth of the at-bat. The payoff pitch is swung and put into play but fielded by Ramírez who gloves it and throws to Lindor to get Kinsler as Lindor makes the turn for a double play! Nick Castellanos bats as the designated hitter and faces Tomlin with the bases empty. He waits for the first pitch, and Castellanos swings and hits a fly ball to the rookie, Greg Allen, in center field who makes the grab for out number three. So in Tomlin's first inning back from the DL, he attacks the strike zone very well. No strikeouts but nobody is left on base, and the score stays 1–0 Indians after one inning.

Carlos Santana, the first baseman, leads off the second inning batting for the first time. Bell's pitch and Santana swings and grounds out slowly to Jeimer Candelario at third, who throws Santana out, sprinting to first. Yandy Díaz, defending at third base today, bats with one out. When Diaz has been called to play, he has delivered. Chad Bell pitches with a 0–2 count, the pitch, and Díaz swings and lines a sharp single to left for a base hit. Brandon Guyer is the batter with Yandy Díaz on first with one out and a 1–0 lead. Chad Bell makes his pitch, and Guyer hits another single to Mahtook in left for a hit. Díaz stops at second base, and now batting with two men on is the catcher Roberto Pérez. Pérez steps to the plate with one out and base runners covering first and second. Bell could use a ground ball double play, or he will take a strikeout as he has Pérez down, 0–2. The pitch, and Pérez hits a single into left field as the Tribe's third base coach, Mike Sarbaugh, sends Díaz home, who slides in headfirst as Mikie Mahtook's throw is cut off and the Indians go up, 2–0, with three straight singles hit into left field. Pérez records RBI number 30, and the Indians look to do more damage. With Pérez on first and Guyer on second with one out, Greg Allen gets a free pass that loads the bases for Francisco Lindor.

Chad Bell is struggling to find a good rhythm with his pitches and is now behind Frankie Lindor with a 3–1 count; he is in danger of walking home a third run. Bell's offering is grounded to Ian Kinsler, who gets the force out at second, while Brandon Guyer comes home to make it 3–0 Indians. Lindor beats the throw at first, and the Tigers couldn't get the double play. The Tribe's shortstop doesn't hit it hard, but he gets the job done with an infield fielder's choice.

Austin Jackson is next up with runners at the corners for Cleveland with two outs. The Tigers are in danger of letting this game get out of hand early. Jackson bats with a 2–2 count and grounds out to short-stop José Iglesias to retire the Indians, but two more runs are tallied. The Tigers come to bat in the bottom of the second inning down by three. Josh Tomlin returns to the mound with a bit of a margin for error and will face first baseman, John Hicks, with a 3–0 lead. After working the count to one ball and two strikes on Hicks, here is the pitch, strike three called! Hicks looks at a fastball and doesn't even move his bat for out number one as Tomlin gets his first strikeout.

Mikie Mahtook bats for the first time, and trailing by three, he wants to get something started. Tomlin's pitch, he delivers ball one and it is a 1–0 count. On Tomlin's second pitch to Mahtook, he swings, and Lindor scoops the ball up and throws to Santana for the second out. Jeimer Candelario will bat with the bases empty. The first pitch to Candelario and the ball is hit, and is deflected off Lindor's glove and into left field for a two-out single. Jacoby Jones bats now with runners on first and second after James McCann drove a single to Guyer in right with two outs. Tomlin makes the 1–2 pitch to Jones, and he swings and smokes an RBI single into center field. Candelario scores to make it 3–1 Indians, and the Tigers are clawing their way back with some clutch two-out hitting. Three straight two-out hits reduce the Tribe lead down to two, and Mickey Callaway, the Tribe's pitching coach, will have a talk with Tomlin. The short-stop, José Iglesias, flies out to Greg Allen in center field for the third out, but the Tigers make it a 3–1 ball game after two innings played in Detroit.

In the top of the third inning, José Ramírez leads off for Cleveland. Ramírez is 1–1 with a solo home run to left field that Mikie Mahtook knocked over the wall with his bare hand when he tried to make a play. Chad Bell is ahead of Ramírez with a 0–2 count. The pitch, he swings, and this ball is lined to the gap in left center field for a hit. Ramírez rounds first for a hustle stand-up double, his league leading forty-fifth double of the season. With no outs, Edwin Encarnacion bats; he is 0–1 facing Bell today, but Encarnacion is batting now with Ramírez in scoring position. Bell's 2–1 pitch and

Encarnacion grounds this ball to the third baseman, Candelario, who decides to get Encarnacion and doesn't stop Ramírez from coming to third. You've really got to wonder about that decision, not looking the runner back. Instead, he is off the base, and Jeimer Candelario, who is not going to have time to field the ball and run to third, doesn't look the runner back, and Cleveland moves José Ramírez ninety-feet closer to home. So with one out, Carlos Santana steps to the plate with his chance at an RBI if he can score Ramírez. This will be Chad Bell's sixty-first pitch in two and one-third innings.

"The pitch, swung on, a slow chopper to the mound coming home with the throw is Bell, head first slide, safe is Ramírez! He slapped home plate with his left hand before McCann got the tag down. I don't know how José scored from third," Tom Hamilton comments.

It is 4–1 Indians as Carlos Santana is safe at first base with an RBI since Ramírez slides home and beats the tag. Well, it isn't a bad decision by Chad Bell, but you just don't expect the runner to go home on a ball that just barely reaches the mound. Tip your cap to Ramírez for outstanding and aggressive baserunning. Yandy Díaz grounds out into an inning ending four-six-three double play as Santana is forced at second base, but after two and a half innings, the Indians lead the Tigers 4–1, taking the run back that they gave up. It is now the bottom of the fourth inning with the Indians leading their division rival by a score of 4–1. Tomlin faces Tigers' first baseman, John Hicks, who struck out in his only at-bat. The 3–1 pitch and Tomlin's pitch is high and wide as the Tigers get a leadoff base runner on Tomlin's first walk. Tomlin is not known for walking many batters, but when he does, he has a reputation of keeping them stranded. Mikie Mahtook is now the batter with a runner on first; Mahtook is 0–1 facing Tomlin with a groundout. On the two-strike pitch, Mahtook swings, and the ball is grounded and fielded by Lindor who gets Hicks at second as José Ramírez turns two, a double play! It is the second double play turned by the Tribe defense, and Tomlin's leadoff walk does no damage. Very nice play on the turn by both Lindor and Ramírez to get the double play; you never want to see a ball dropped or bobbled, and they play this very well.

Josh Tomlin gets the third baseman, Candelario, to fly out on a ball smoked directly at Guyer for the third out. The Tigers plate no runners, and Tomlin keeps rolling. It is now the top half of the fifth inning with the Indians leading the Tigers, 4–1, and José Ramírez the batter. The Clevelanders get a leadoff base hit to center field by Austin Jackson. Chad Bell offers his pitch, and Ramírez swings and shoots this ball far down the left field line and into the corner. Austin Jackson flies from first to third, and Ramírez is now 3–3 with a home run and two doubles off Chad Bell. The bases are juiced now with only one out as Encarnacion reaches first base with a four-pitch walk, and Santana lines out to Ian Kinsler at second for the first out. Yandy Díaz will bat with a golden opportunity to put this game away with his team already leading by three. The Tigers decide to make a pitching move; Zac Reininger comes on for Bell, who has given up four runs and is responsible for all three runners on base. Díaz awaits the 1–0 pitch from Reininger; Diaz swings and lines a laser over the mound and into center for an RBI base hit! The pitcher has to duck out of the way because Díaz lines a bullet up the middle that scores Jackson and advances Ramírez to third and Encarnacion to second. Now it is 5–1 Indians in the fifth, and one run is all they would get as Guyer gets called out on the infield fly rule, and Pérez lines out to second base.

It is the home half of the fifth inning in Detroit and the score is 5–1 with the Indians in the lead. Tiger's catcher, James McCann, leads off with a single to Austin Jackson into left, and for the second inning in a row, the Tigers get their leadoff man aboard. Jacoby Jones is now the batter; he is 1–1 with the Tigers' only hit that scored a run. Here's the pitch, it is a grounder to Lindor, and they do it again! Lindor forces out McCann at second, and Ramírez throws out Jones for the third twin killer of the ball game! Well, Tomlin looks strong after five innings as he gets Iglesias to groundout to retire the Tigers in the fifth. After five innings, Tomlin has allowed just the one run in his first game back. We move to the top of the sixth inning, and Zac Reininger who replaced Chad Bell gets Greg Allen looking at strike three for his first strikeout. Francisco Lindor bats with one out; he is hitless in three at-bats but has been productive defensively, helping to turn three double plays.

"The 1–1 pitch, swung on this is hammered deep right field this ball is gone! Francisco Lindor hits number twenty-six. A blast to right and the Indians lead it six to one," Tom Hamilton comments.

The Indians add another run, making them grand slam proof as they now have a five-run lead in the sixth inning. With that home run, Frankie Lindor becomes the first shortstop in Cleveland Indians' history to hit twenty-six home runs in a season as he passes Asdrúbal Cabrera! The Indians get a one-out base hit into left by Austin Jackson, who notches his second hit of the game, and now José Ramírez is the batter and is currently batting one thousand in today's game with two doubles and a home run.

"Pitch to him, and he sends a drive, deep right field, this ball near the wall leaping is Presley and this ball is gone! It's a two-run home run for José Ramírez! He has two home runs, he has two doubles!" Tom Hamilton announces.

On both home runs for Ramírez, one to left field and this one to right, the fielder knocks the baseball over the wall! What Ramírez did in the first inning where Mahtook hit the ball over the wall with his hand, Alex Presley does the same thing with his glove! Just when you thought you'd never see that again, it happens twice in one game. On both home runs hit by Ramírez, tip your cap to the Tiger outfielders for assisting him both times. The Indians now lead by seven, 8–1 Tribe as Ramírez just hit his twenty-second homer of the season. So it is the bottom of the sixth inning, and the Detroit Tigers have a mountain of runs to climb, but with this pitching staff, you are really going to need to catch some breaks. With the Tribe in front, 8–1, Tomlin has allowed just the one run on five hits. Ian Kinsler bats with a full count. The pitch, and strike three is called on Ian Kinsler! He can't believe it as he starts to jog to first, but he gets called out by the home plate umpire. Josh Tomlin gets his second strikeout, and there is one out in the Tiger sixth. With two gone now, Nick Castellanos gets a base hit to Greg Allen in center field, just the Tigers sixth hit of the game, all singles. After that hit, Terry Francona goes to the mound and says, "Job well done," as he relieves Tomlin, who pitches five and two-thirds innings with two strikeouts on his first appearance since July 30.

Reliever Nick Goody comes on to pitch; he faces John Hicks with two outs. Goody works quickly, and the pitch is swung on and missed for strike three! Three pitches, three strikes, and the Tigers strand a runner as Hicks strikes out for a second time. It is the top of the eighth inning now with the Indians in command, 8–1. Leading off is José Ramírez, who is 4–4 with two home runs and two doubles on the day. The Tigers have pitcher Daniel Norris on the mound working with a full count as he readies to toss his ninth pitch of the at-bat. The pitch and this ball is smoked to deep center field. Racing back is Jones, and the ball carries over his head and to the wall for another extra base hit for Ramírez! On a full count nine-pitch at-bat, José once again hits it hard, and he is five for five today with two homers and three doubles! He is the first Cleveland Indian to get an extra base hit in all five at-bats since Kelly Shoppach in 2008. What a job today by José Ramírez getting an extra base hit in all five of his at-bats!

The Indians' decision makers call on Giovanny Urshela to be the pinch runner at second base. Edwin Encarnacion bats with nobody out; he is 0–3 in four at-bats with a walk. Daniel Norris makes the 2–1 offering, and Encarnacion yanks this ball far down the line in left and all the way to the wall for an RBI double to make it 9–1 Indians. Urshela, the pinch runner, scores from second base, and the Tribe continues to add to their already padded lead. We go to the bottom of the ninth inning in an 11–1 ball game; the Indians score once more in the eighth on a bases-loaded walk to score their tenth run. Then Lonnie Chisenhall doubles in the ninth to score Urshela to make it a ten-run lead over the Tigers. Dan Otero is the new pitcher for Cleveland and faces Efrén Navarro. The pitch and a base hit into left field to start the bottom of the ninth. But Dan Otero gets John Hicks to line out to Abe Almonte in left field, and the Indians are two outs away from winning their eleventh straight game. Mikie Mahtook steps in as the batter with one out and a runner on first but down by ten runs.

"He sets and fires, a swing and a double play ball to short. Urshela to second one, González' relay to first double play, ball game! The Indians turn their fifth double play. So if there was anything the Indians didn't do well today, good luck finding it. The Indians demolish the Tigers today eleven to one," Tom Hamilton comments.

Josh Tomlin is the winning pitcher in his first game coming off the disabled list. The Indians have won eleven straight games, three shy of tying the club record. The Indians are twenty-four games above .500 80–56. The Tribe leaves the Motor City tonight and will play in Chicago before going back to Cleveland.

Chapter 4

---◆◆◆ ◆◆◆---

Sox Hung Out to Dry, Games 12–15

From Guaranteed Rate Field in Chicago, Illinois, we have the Cleveland Indians battling the Chicago White Sox. It is a four-game series for the Indians that will wrap up their eleven-game road trip. The Indians sit alone at the top of the American League Central, 25.5 games above the White Sox who sit in last place. Of the last twelve games counting today, eight have been against a division rival. The White Sox come into this game after beating the Tampa Bay Rays in a three-game series, taking games 2 and 3 here at home. The scalding hot Indians begin this series with an eleven-game win streak, taking the final game from Boston, three from Kansas City, three in New York, and four in Detroit. James Shields will get the start for his club facing Francisco Lindor; Shields is 2–5 with an ERA above five. The first pitch is high for a ball, and we are underway in the Windy City.

Lindor smokes the 1–0 pitch to short; Tim Anderson plays it on one hop and retires Lindor for the first out. James Shields strikes out Austin Jackson, who gets called out on strikes; he has only delivered eight pitches, and the Indians have two fast outs. Lonnie Chisenhall, the Indians' right fielder, tonight steps up with Ramírez on base, who took a free pass. Chisenhall is down, 0–2; he swings at the next pitch and sends a ball to medium deep left field, and Rymer Liriano grabs it for the third out. The Indians make no noise in the first inning, and José Ramírez is left stranded on base. Trevor Bauer starts game 1 for the Indians; a win today would give him his fifteenth win on the season. Chicago second baseman, Alen Hanson, swings aggressively at the first pitch and sharply grounds out to Ramírez covering second base. The second batter is third baseman, Yolmer Sánchez; Bauer's first pitch is a strike, and he gets ahead, 0–1. Trevor Bauer's last start was in the Bronx, and it was the first game of the doubleheader in which the Indians beat the Yankees, 2–1. He pitched six innings and struck out four batters. Sánchez is down, 1–2, and Bauer delivers his next offering, and the ball nails Sanchez in the elbow for a hit batter. Sánchez takes first base, and José Abreu will bat with a man on.

Bauer moves into the motion and tosses a ball out of the zone for a 1–0 count. The next pitch and Abreu swings and sends a pop-up near third base as Yandy Díaz grabs the floater for the second out. Avisaíl García steps in with two gone and Sánchez the baserunner at first. Sanchez takes a good lead as Bauer glances and then delivers the pitch. The first offering is swung on and missed, and García falls behind, 0–1. Bauer checks the runner again, here's his pitch, and it is fouled back at the plate. No balls, two strikes is the count; Trevor Bauer with the wind and pitch as Sánchez sprints for second, but the batter Garcia takes a swing and a miss! Bauer's first strikeout ends the first inning, and the White Sox leave a runner stranded, and this game is scoreless after one inning. The leadoff batter for Cleveland is Carlos Santana to start the second frame in this scoreless game. James Shields falls behind Santana; the count is 3–1.

"The pitch, swung on lifted high in the air to deep right center, this ball is gone! Carlos Santana hits number twenty-two and the Indians just keep rocking on the road," Tom Hamilton announces.

Santana's leadoff homer puts the Tribe up 1–0, and for the twelfth game in a row, the Indians score first! Third baseman Yandy Díaz bats next. The pitch, and Díaz lines a ball deep to right and off the wall beyond Avisaíl García for a double. The first out is recorded as Abe Almonte swings and hits a third ball to right field, but this ball will be caught by Garcia and Diaz remains at second base. The designated hitter, Francisco Mejía, who plays catcher in the minors, will take his swings batting with one away. Mejía swings at the first pitch, but he is a little late on that heater. With a hurler tossing ninety-seven miles per hour, you need to show patients when you're a rookie. Shield's pitch and Mejía swings and grounds out to second baseman, Alen Hanson, for the second out while Díaz moves over to third base. Roberto Pérez steps in the batter's box with two outs, a man on third and his club leading by a run. On a full-count pitch, Pérez swings and smokes this ball down the line in left. The ball kicks up chalk for a fair ball, and coming home on the two out RBI double is Yandy Díaz to make it 2–0 Indians! We'll get him on, get him over and get him in.

The rookie's productive out moves up his teammate from second to third base, and Roberto Pérez with the RBI stays smoking hot in two out situations. Francisco Lindor hits into his second ground-out, and Matt Davidson plays it himself and runs to first base, and the inning is over. It is 2–0, and the Indians lead Chicago, heading to the White Sox half of this inning. First baseman Matt Davidson starts off the second with a ground ball base hit that finds its way into center field for Chicago's first hit. The man behind the dish, Omar Narváez, steps up, swinging for the first time, and he is the tying run at the plate. Davidson is the runner at first base. Trevor Bauer delivers a first pitch strike to Narváez, a snap throw by Pérez to first, and Davidson is almost caught leaning too far. The Indians with a two-run advantage, and Bauer delivers the pitch. Narváez swings and smokes a line drive into center field but right into the glove of Jackson for the out. The seventh man in the Sox lineup, Tim Anderson, steps in for his first at-bat; he wants to put a good swing on the ball and tie this game up. He certainly has power in his bat.

Bauer works ahead of Anderson, 1–2, and is looking for a second strikeout. He makes the pitch, a swing, and a miss at a ball in the dirt! So two down, and Davidson is still at first base, and Rymer Liriano is batting next. Liriano works the count full, and on that last pitch, he nearly ties this game with a home run, but the ball slices foul. Trevor Bauer gets the sign and offers the 3–2 pitch, another swing, and a miss on a high fastball! Bauer racks up three strikeouts; two in the inning, and we move ahead to the top of the fourth inning in Chicago. Carlos Santana leads off the top half of the fourth; he is 1–1 with a leadoff homer in the second. James Shields has struck out two and given up two earned runs. The pitch, and

Santana swings and grounds the ball into center field for his second leadoff hit. Yandy Díaz is now the batter; he is 1–1 with a double and a run scored today as he came home on the two out RBI double by Roberto Pérez. Santana remains on first with nobody out, and Díaz batting with a 3–1 count, he swings and lines the ball right into the glove of Tim Anderson. The shortstop snatches it just before the ball hits the dirt on the infield, and the Indians have one out.

The left fielder, Abe Almonte, comes up to bat, and he takes a first pitch strike from James Shields. Almonte is looking to find a hole in the defense to advance or score the runner. Santana streaks to second on the pitch, which is swung and chopped slowly to first, but that will advance the runner, although now there are two outs. Francisco Mejía steps in; he is 0–1 on the day with a groundout. Carlos Santana is the two out base runner on second. Shields offers the 1–0 pitch; a swing and the ball is smashed into center field for a hit! Santana will score to make it 3–0 Cleveland on the first big league hit and RBI by Francisco Mejía! What a moment for the young man; it must be a great feeling getting that first hit out of the way.

The ball gets tossed to the Indian's dugout, and the team steps onto the field, giving him a well-deserved hand. Roberto Pérez strikes out to end the inning, but the Tribe scores a third run on the first major league hit by Francisco Mejía. The score is now 3–0 Indians after three and a half innings in Chicago. José Abreu leads off the bottom half of the inning; the White Sox have banged out only one hit off Bauer, who has struck out five. The first offering is high for ball 1 to Abreu; he is hitless today with a pop-out. The second pitch by Bauer to José Abreu and he chops the ball to Lindor, who plays it on a bounce and makes the throw in time to Santana for the out. Avisaíl García faces Bauer for a second time; Bauer fanned García the first time they faced each other today, and the Indians hurler has five strikeouts on the day. Pérez calls for the pitch, and there is another swing and a miss! García chases a fastball near his head, and that whiff gives Bauer six in this game!

Matt Davidson gets his second at-bat; he has the White Sox only base hit as Trevor Bauer has set down eight straight since then. Bauer is bidding for a seventh strikeout as Davidson is down in the count, 1–2. Here it comes, strike three called! Trevor Bauer catches Davidson looking at a breaking ball that falls right over the plate, and Davidson does not offer. The Indians do not score in the fifth inning, Francisco Lindor gets thrown out trying for a double, and Austin Jackson is robbed of a home run to straightaway center field on a liner caught by Adam Engel. In the bottom of the inning, the Sox's shortstop, Tim Anderson, gets aboard on a one out single that is smoked into left field; now Rymer Liriano is the batter, and he is hitless today with a swinging strikeout. Trevor Bauer falls behind, throwing three straight balls, but he has not allowed a walk so far today. The pitch is swung on, and Liriano drives this ball deep to left; it is a two-run home run, and the Tribe lead is now cut to 3–2 in the fifth. That is just the third hit allowed by Trevor Bauer, but it brings the Sox within a run. Bauer thought he would try and get Liriano to swing at a breaking ball on a 3–0 pitch, but it doesn't fool him.

It is now Cleveland's half of the seventh inning, and the Tribe still leads the White Sox by a score of 3–2. Abraham Almonte steps in for his third at-bat and takes a walk to begin the seventh. The rookie designated hitter, Francisco Mejía, is the batter; he got his first big league hit and RBI on a base hit to center field in the fourth inning that gave the Indians a 3–0 lead. The 1–0 pitch is swung on and lined back at Shields, who couldn't get his glove up in time and gets whacked by the ball as it ricochets back toward home plate. The catcher Narváez throws out Mejía, and Almonte advances to second base. The White Sox are forced to change pitchers after James Shields gets drilled in the knee on a line drive off the bat of Francisco Mejía. Reliever Jake Petricka will take over with one out and his team down by a run. The first batter he faces is the Indians catcher, and Petricka strikes out Roberto Pérez for the second out, bringing Lindor to the plate. Frankie Lindor is hoping to come through for his team, as they are only leading by a run as he awaits the 1–2 pitch from Petricka. The two-strike pitch is made, and Lindor swings and smokes a single into right field. Almonte is waved home, and the Indians get a much-needed insurance run and are now leading, 4–2.

Lindor's second hit of the game gives him seventy RBIs on the year! As we move to the bottom of the seventh, it is 4–2 Indians with the lead, and Trevor Bauer faces Omar Narváez as Bauer is closing in on one hundred pitches. Bauer delivers a swing and sharp ground ball to first that is ruled fair, and Santana grabs it and flips to Bauer, covering for the out. That is great awareness by Carlos Santana as he prevents what would have been a leadoff double by Omar Narváez. After six and one-third innings of baseball pitched by Trevor Bauer, Francona decides it is time to make a pitching change. Trevor Bauer exits after giving up two runs, three hits while he strikes out nine! A one out single by Tim Anderson and a double by Liriano makes this a 4–3 ball game as Joe smith surrenders a crucial run. Rymer Liriano has all three of Chicago's RBIs, and it is now the top of the eighth inning with the Indians lead cut down to a single run again.

A new pitcher enters for the White Sox as Chris Beck takes over for Jake Petricka, who tosses two-thirds of an inning and gives up no runs. As the game winds down its still 4–3, the Indians have the lead late in this game. José Ramírez will bat, leading off the top of the eighth inning, he is 0 for 2 with a walk. Beck's first pitch is taken for a strike.

"The 0–1 swung on, this is hit a ton deep right field, this ball is gone! Clears the bullpen and into the seats in right and José Ramírez keeps pummeling the baseball," Tom Hamilton says.

Ramírez now has accounted for twenty-three home runs, and for the second time today, the Indians get a leadoff home run! It is now a 5–3 Indians lead, and twice the White Sox cut the lead down to a run, and the Indians bats respond. As we move to the bottom of the ninth inning, the score remains Cleveland 5, Chicago 3. The White Sox are down to their final out but have two runners on base. Cody Allen gave up two walks, and a runner is retired on a force out. Pinch hitter Rob Brantly will bat for the center fielder, Adam Engel. Cody Allen is searching for his twenty-fourth save of the season if he could just keep the runners stranded. The Sox's Brantly is down, 1–2, trying to get a clutch hit with two men on and the Indians' streak in jeopardy. He is the potential winning run at the plate.

As the next pitch is offered, it is "a swing and a miss, ball game! Chased the curveball in the dirt, Allen strikes out Brantly, the Indians have now won twelve in a row! Trevor Bauer gets his fifteenth win and Cody Allen gets save number twenty-four. The Indians keep rolling, they beat the White Sox today by a final score of five to three" (Tom Hamilton). The numbers for Cleveland go beyond the twelve straight wins. They have won twenty-one of the last twenty-five contests and have won each of the last eighteen games when they have scored first. The Tribe is 69–14 when they score four or more runs per contest.

During the post-game, Manager Terry Francona is quizzed about his thoughts on the twelve-game win streak. "We'll show up tomorrow and try and win again. What happened ten, twelve days ago doesn't matter. Just we'll show up tomorrow and see if we can beat the White Sox. That's the best way to go about it."

In the clubhouse, Tribe's second baseman, José Ramírez, comments on the streak as well. "I see the team feeling the same way. Were happy, we're relaxed, we're having a good time, we're united, and that's something that's really important."

From Guaranteed Rate Field on the south side of Chicago, it is the Chicago White Sox hosting the Cleveland Indians. It is game number 2 of this four-game series, and there is nothing more exciting in baseball than a good rivalry, and these two ball clubs have been Central Division rivals since 1994. The Indians are playing in the city of baseball's defending champions. In 2016, the White Sox National League neighbor, the Chicago Cubs, beat the Indians in game 7 of the World Series in Cleveland. It is the first baseball championship for Chicago since the White Sox swept the World Series in 2005 but the first time the Cubs franchise were crowned champions since 1908. It is September baseball, and despite the letdown in last year's Fall Classic, with the way the Tribe has been playing, they are heavy favorites to make it back there again. The Indians are dominating the central with a team record of 81–56, winning twelve consecutive games, including eight on the road. Today's starting pitcher for the White Sox is David Holmberg, and Frankie Lindor will lead off for the Tribe. The first pitch called a strike, and we are underway in Chicago. Now the 0–2 pitch, and Lindor swings and sends a ball to shallow center field, and making the grab is Adam Engel.

Austin Jackson is the batter; in recent games when he has played, he has been prone to strikeout and not be as productive at the plate as he would like to be. With an even 2–2 count on Jackson, the next pitch is on its way. "He delivers, and it's swung on and hammered into deep center field, Engel on the run…it's gone to dead center! Austin Jackson has hit his seventh home run. Oh, did he pound that one to straightaway center," Tom Hamilton comments. That tally marks the thirteenth straight game where the Indians score first! A solo homer by Austin Jackson gives the Tribe a 1–0 lead in the top of the first inning. Jackson was robbed of a home run in yesterday's 5–3 victory, but he makes up for it today with a first inning dinger as the Sox Engel couldn't run that one down.

José Ramírez bats next; he has had a very productive road trip with five home runs so far. David Holmmberg makes his 1–0 pitch to Ramírez. "Swung on, this is hit high, this is hit deep to left. Back goes Liriano, track, wall, gone! Well we told you the ball carries here and back to back jacks by Jackson and now Ramírez and the Indians lead two to nothing," announces Tom Hamilton. The Indians again waste no time taking the lead and then building on it with two solo home runs on the first nine pitches made by David Holmberg. That is the sixth home run by Ramírez on this road trip, and his bat stays smoking hot! The next three batters for the Indians reach base. Edwin Encarnacion lines a single into left field, and Carlos Santana and Yandy Díaz both reach with a walk. The right fielder, Brandon Guyer, is the batter, and the bases are loaded with just one out. Guyer falls behind, 1–2, here's the pitch, and he hits this ball sharply to Tim Anderson at short, but his only play is at second, and Edwin Encarnacion scores on the force out. A three-run first inning for the Indians and they have runners at the corners with two outs.

The Indians are finally retired in the top of the first when Greg Allen strikes out swinging. As we move to the bottom of the first inning, Danny Salazar takes the hill to pitch for the first time since coming off the disabled list. He has been handed a solid three-run lead to work with. Salazar faces the third baseman, Yolmer Sánchez, and he walks him on seven pitches. The next batter, Yoán Moncada, playing second base today, falls behind Salazar, 1–2. Salazar makes his pitch as the runner Sanchez breaks for second, a swing, and a miss by Moncada. Yan Gomes tries to make the throw to second, but his attempt is off target and skips into center field. Yolmer Sánchez springs up and advances to third on the throwing error by Gomes. A strikeout and an error give Chicago a good scoring opportunity, and José Abreu will be the batter. Abreu is in a good position with a 3–0 count, and Salazar is struggling early with command and already has one walk. The 3–0 pitch, Abreu swings and chops the ball to Ramírez, who retires Abreu on the groundout, but it is a 3–1 ball game as Yolmer Sánchez comes home on the ball put in play. It was that throwing error by Gomes that cost the Indians a run.

Danny Salazar is really struggling to find good command with his pitches. Avisaíl García heads to first base on the second walk allowed by Salazar this inning. The Indians send pitching coach Mickey Callaway to have a chat with Salazar; they want to be sure everything is okay. Three runs to one and the Indians lead in the first, but Rob Brantly represents the tying run as he steps up to bat with Avisaíl García on first base. The Indians are already warming up the bullpen in case this gets out of hand. Salazar makes the first pitch, and Rob Brantly tries to spin away, but the pitch hits him. Now make that three base runners for the White Sox this inning, all who have reached without getting a hit. Two walks and a hit batter have given Chicago a chance to do some early damage. Yolmer Sánchez was the first walked batter, and he scored on the groundout by José Abreu. There are two runners on base for Matt Davidson; his team trails by two in this first inning. Davidson falls behind in the count and awaits the two-strike pitch. Salazar is into the motion, and Davidson swings and hammers this ball to deep center, and this ball is gone! A three-run home run by Matt Davidson gives the White Sox a 4–3 lead, and for the first time in over sixty-seven innings, the Indians are behind on the scoreboard.

Terry Francona has seen enough, so he comes out to give Salazar the early hook. Nick Goody would replace Dany Salazar, who pitches just two-thirds of an inning in his first game back. For the Indians, this will be a game of relief pitchers, and if they are going to win, the relievers will be asked to pitch eight and one-third innings or more.

Tim Anderson and Rymer Liriano are the third and fourth batters to reach this inning via the walk. Chicago leads by one run with two men on, and Adam Engel is the ninth man to bat this inning. Goody's pitch and Engel sends a fly ball to Jackson in left field to end the inning. With a score of 4–3, the White Sox have the lead over the Indians, heading to the top of the second inning in Chicago. Francisco Lindor leads off with the team trailing in this game; that is one thing we haven't seen much in the last twelve games. The last time the Indians were behind in a game was at Yankee Stadium on August 28, and it is now September 5. Lindor today is 0–1, and he lined out to center in the first inning. David Holmberg's fourth pitch to Lindor is high and wide for a walk, and the Indians bring the go-ahead run in Austin Jackson to the plate. Jackson is 1–1 so far in this game; he hit the front end of the back to back home runs, and José Ramírez follows suit. The pitch by Holmberg, Austin Jackson smokes this ball to short, and Tim Anderson and Yoán Moncada turn the double play, and there are two outs. José Ramírez bats with the bases empty after the double play is turned.

"Now the 2–2, breaking ball swung on blasted deep left center, this game is tied! A hanging breaking ball and José Ramírez has done it again! He had one the other day in Detroit and he has done it again here tonight," Tom Hamilton comments.

That is the third time on this road trip José Ramírez has a multihomer game. He hit two in game one against the Yankees. He did it twice at Detroit in game four when he had the big five for five day, and tonight he ties the game at four with his third multihomer game. The Indians as a team have hit seventeen home runs on this road trip, and Ramírez has hit seven of them. We are in the bottom of the second inning, and it is a brand-new ball game. The Indians fell behind the White Sox by a run in the first but retie the game on Ramírez's home run. The Indians make another pitching change as Dan Otero replaces Nick Goody, who pitches one-third of a scoreless first inning. Dany Salazar had a very rough start, so the bullpen will try and carry the load for the remainder of the game. Dan Otero is pitching to Yolmer Sánchez, who scored on the groundout by José Abreu that made it 3–1. The payoff pitch by Otero, a swing and a miss! He chases the fastball away for the first out. Dan Otero does a nice job setting down the White Sox, and they get one hit but leave no men on base. Carlos Santana leads off the third inning in this 4–4 ball game; he is 0–0 reaching base with a walk. The pitch and Carlos Santana swings and hits a slow roller to third. Yolmer Sánchez has no play as he is playing normal depth, and it is a lucky break for the Tribe as Santana gets on board with an infield hit. Yandy Díaz is the batter, he also was walked by the pitcher his first time up. Holmberg offers the 2–2 pitch, and Díaz swings, and another ball hit to the third baseman, Sánchez retires Díaz on the throw to first base, and Santana moves into scoring position with one out.

Brandon Guyer crouches in to bat; he drove in the Tribe's third run on a groundout in the first inning. On the first pitch, Guyer is hit, and the Indians have runners on first and second as Yan Gomes steps in for his second at-bat. David Holmberg gets ahead of Gomes, 0–2, but on the two-strike pitch, Gomes swings and taps another ball that hits slowly to third base. Yolmer Sánchez snatches the ball and steps on third to get Santana just before he throws to first, but Gomes hustles down the line and beats it out. Guyer moves to second base on the force, and now the two out batter will be Greg Allen. This game remains tied at four in the top of this third inning, and Allen is hitless with a strikeout his first plate appearance. With a count of one ball, one strike on Greg Allen, Brandon Guyer is the go-ahead runner on second base, and Gomes the runner on first. The pitch, Greg Allen swings and yanks this ball fair by Sánchez and into the corner in left for extra bases. Brandon Guyer scores, and right behind him is Yan Gomes scoring all the way from first! Greg Allen makes the turn toward third, and he is caught in a rundown and is tagged out. But the Indians score twice to take a 6–4 lead on the two out double by Greg Allen!

It is now the top half of the ninth inning, and the Indians have a 6–4 lead over the White Sox. Yan Gomes is the batter, two men on and two men out. Gomes scored in the third inning on the double to left by Greg Allen. Pitching for the Pale Hose is Chris Beck, trying to keep the score the way it is to give his hitters a chance. First pitch, "Yan Gomes sends a long fly ball, deep left field, Liriano back he's out of room it's out of here! Yan Gomes with a two out three run-homer in the ninth opens up some breathing room for the Tribe. It's now a 9–4 Cleveland lead! Gomes with his eleventh home run of the season and that gives him forty-nine runs batted in," comments Matt Underwood. As we move to the bottom of the ninth inning, the Indians lead this game 9–4 and what a job by the Tribe bullpen today. The Indians have relied on their relievers since the first inning when Danny Salazar served up four runs that gave the White Sox the lead. Shawn Armstrong is the Indians' seventh relief pitcher of the day as Cody Allen gets the night off in this nonsave situation. Matt Davidson is batting; he is 1–4 with a three-run home run that came back in the bottom of the first against Salazar.

"The one two pitch, swing and a miss, ball game! Got him with a slider and the Indians make it thirteen consecutive wins, one shy of the club record set a year ago. The Indians beat up the Sox again. The final tonight—Cleveland nine and Chicago four as the Indians reduce their magic number to fourteen," Tom Hamilton announces.

The Cleveland Indians' eleven-game road trip is winding down as they play game three of four against the White Sox before they head back to Cleveland. What a road trip it has been; they started off in the Big Apple and swept the Yankees in a three-game series. Then they traveled to Detroit and pounded their rivals in all four games, outscoring the Tigers, 29–5. They play the White Sox today and tomorrow as the Indians have a two-wins-to-none lead in this series and a chance to repeat some history! In 2016, the Cleveland Indians got on a hot streak and won fourteen straight games from June 17 to July 1. When the Indians started this road trip on August 28, they had a six-and-a-half game lead over the Minnesota Twins. Now they have widened the gap by four and a half more games to an eleven-game cushion.

Reynaldo López takes to the mound in game number three for Chicago, facing the leadoff batter, Francisco Lindor. A three-pitch at-bat sets down Lindor as he grounds out to the second baseman, Alen Hanson, to start this ball game. The right fielder, Lonnie Chisenhall, is batting second in this game; he's usually hitting deeper in the lineup but there must be something Terry Francona senses in moving him up in the lineup as an advantage for his team. The pitch, and Chisenhall swings and hits a ball beyond the infield and into center field for a one-out base hit. José Ramírez gets aboard due to a miscue by the first baseman. Both runners move into scoring position, but the Indians do not capitalize on the opportunity. Edwin Encarnacion and Carlos Santana both fly out to end the top of the first, and the White Sox come to bat. Carlos Carrasco will pitch for the Indians in this third game. Over these last thirteen games, the Indians pitching staff from the starter to the closer have been on another level, and Carrasco looks to continue that dominance in this game. His last start was in Detroit where he pitched seven complete innings and gave up just one run on six hits, but Cody Allen was credited with the win. Second baseman, Alen Hanson, leads off for the Sox as he swings and skies the ball on the infield; Francisco Lindor calls for it and cradles it for the first out. The second man to bat is Yolmer Sánchez, and Carrasco pitches to him with an even 2–2 count. The pitch, swing, and a miss! Sánchez chases the high cutter, and Carrasco gets his first strikeout!

José Abreu, the designated hitter, steps to the plate with the bases empty after two quick outs were recorded on just seven pitches by Carrasco. Abreu is in a two-strike hole, the 0–2 pitch, strike three called! A slider placed nicely on the outer half of the plate, and Abreu doesn't offer at it. A good first inning for Carlos Carrasco, he makes only ten pitches and strikes out two of the first three batters that he faces. Yandy Díaz gets a leadoff walk to begin the second inning for the Indians. He moves up to third after the one out double hit to right field by Tyler Naquin. With one out, there are runners on second and third for the catcher Roberto Pérez. Reynaldo López has Pérez down, 1–2, but he needs to be careful. Pérez has swung a hot bat lately with men on base. Here comes his pitch and called strike 3. Pérez is in disbelief, shaking his head as he walks back to the Indian's dugout. Two on and two gone for Lindor, who is 0–1 so far with a groundout. Lindor swings on an even count and pops a ball up that is drifting to the third base side in foul territory, but Sánchez catches it to retire the side, and the Tribe leaves two men on base. That is the second straight inning in which the Indians couldn't score when they had two runners in scoring position with less than two outs.

Avisaíl García, the right fielder, bats in the cleanup spot to begin the bottom of second in this scoreless ball game. García takes the first pitch for a strike. The next pitch by Carrasco, a swing, and a high deep drive to right as Chisenhall races back and makes the grab in front of the wall! Oh, García nearly got that ball over the wall, but it died out there in deep right field for out number one. Nicky Delmonico bats next; he did not play in games 1 and 2 of this series. It is a 1–2 count; the pitch and Delmonico hits a slow roller to Ramírez, who plays it on a bounce, and throws to Santana for the second out. Matt Davidson steps up to bat with two outs and nobody is standing on base. Davidson battles to a full count as he takes the first three pitches for balls and fouls off the next two. Here comes the sixth pitch from Carrasco, he offers and Davidson misses, he swings over the heater! Six batters up, six set down by Carrasco. After two innings, he has three strikeouts! There is no score after two and a half innings played at Guaranteed Rate Field in Chicago as Reynaldo López matches Carlos Carrasco's three-up, three-down inning. Chisenhall hits a slow grounder back to the mound, and Ramírez and Encarnacion are retired on a line out and a pop-out. López has had some struggles in innings 1 and 2, but he has stranded the four base runners that have reached base safely.

As we move to the bottom third of the lineup batting in the home half of the third inning, the White Sox are looking to give their pitcher some run support. Kevan Smith, the man behind the plate, is batting seventh, this is his first at-bat facing Carrasco. Smith swings and makes contact with the 1–0 pitch, and José Ramírez plays the ball on a hop and throws down to first for the out. Tyler Saladino, the shortstop, another new face that did not play in the first two games, gets his first at-bat of the series. Carrasco's first pitch to Saladino, and he swings through it for a first pitch strike. After falling behind, 2–1, Carrasco is back even at two balls and two strikes as Saladino foul tips the fourth pitch. The 2–2 pitch from Carlos Carrasco is swung on and missed! A five-pitch strikeout, Saladino chases a ball in the dirt and chalk up strikeout number four for Cookie! Two batters gone now, and the center fielder, Adam Engel, will take his first hacks. Carrasco gets Engel to fall behind, 0–2. Here's his pitch, and Engel pops the ball near first base, and Carlos Santana grabs it for out number three. Nine White Sox up, nine White Sox down!

Carrasco is looking razor sharp with four strikeouts and all zeros after three innings pitched in the Windy City! Now can the Tribe bats make some noise and get him a run for the next inning? In the top of the fourth, Cleveland's first baseman, Carlos Santana, is batting for the second time today, and he is 0–1 facing López. Santana swings at the 3–2 offering, and this ball falls into left field as Delmonico dives, but the ball nicks off his glove for a hit. Santana makes the turn but would stay at first since the ball never gets away from Delmonico. Yandy Díaz is now the batter; he walked in his first at-bat and was left stranded on base in the second inning. López's pitch, Díaz swings and grounds a single-to-the-right field gap, but Santana holds at second as García cuts the ball off nicely. Abraham Almonte steps to the plate and is quickly down, 0–1, but is looking to drive in Santana from second base with a hit. The pitch is delivered, and the ball gets away from the Sox's catcher, Smith. Santana hustles to third base, and Yandy Díaz decides to hold at first, but now the go-ahead run is just ninety feet from home plate.

López is working behind in the count versus Almonte; the count is 2–1, and Almonte is showing a lot of patience. The next pitch and it is called ball 3, and Smith asks for time to confer with his pitcher. The 3–1 offering to Abe Almonte is called ball 4; the Indians have the bases loaded with nobody out for Tyler Naquin, who doubled but was left stranded his first at-bat. An even 1–1 count as Naquin looks to drive in the game's first run or runs. López delivers, and Naquin sends a deep drive to left field. Delmonico has room for the catch, but Santana scores on the sac fly, and it is a 1–0 Indian's lead. One run is all they get as Roberto Pérez strikes out for a second time, and Lindor remains hitless on a fly out to Nicky Delmonico to end the top half of the fourth. The Indians score first again for the fourteenth game in a row as Carlos Carrasco prepares to go back to work to face the Sox in the bottom half of the inning, clinging to a one-run advantage. The White Sox lineup flips back to the top of the order, and batters one, two, and three will face Carrasco, who is perfect through three innings. Alen Hanson popped out to Lindor in the first inning; he is battling to keep this at-bat alive down, 1–2. Carrasco with four strikeouts, the pitch, a swing, and a miss!

Hanson chases the cutter that is breaking inward toward his knees—that is Carrasco's fifth strikeout! Yolmer Sánchez is the batter, and he steps up for a second time, searching for the team's first hit of this game. Sánchez has fallen behind, 0–2, on Carrasco; he is trying to avoid being whiffed for a second time. Carrasco's two-strike pitch is too low, and the count now goes to one ball, two strikes. It is the bottom of the fourth, and Carrasco to this point has done an amazing job; his pitch count is below fifty. The 1–2 pitch is delivered and swung on and foul-tipped into the glove of Roberto Pérez for Carrasco's sixth strikeout! That is the second time Carrasco strikes out Sánchez, and two batters are gone. The White Sox still have not reached base, and the designated hitter, José Abreu, will try to start a two-out rally. He was called out on strikes his first time up in the first inning. Abreu duels with Carrasco to an even 2–2 count as he waits for the perfect pitch where he can hit the ball into the gap. With nobody on two outs, the pitch, swing, and a miss for strike three! Seven strikeouts for Carlos Carrasco as he strikes out the side; he is still perfect after four innings while only making forty-eight pitches!

As we move to the top of the fifth inning, the Indians threaten but do not score after two two-out singles by Encarnacion and Santana. The score stays 1–0 Cleveland as the White Sox prepare for their at-bats in the bottom half of the inning. The right fielder, Avisaíl García, is the leadoff man facing Carrasco, who is working on a perfect game. The pitch to García, he swings, and there is the Sox's first hit as García smokes a single into center field, and the White Sox have their first baserunner. Nicky Delmonico steps in with a runner at first; he is hitless with a groundout to Ramírez. The 1–0 pitch, Delmonico chops this ball right at Santana, who gloves it on the bounce, steps on first, and then turns and chases García, who is caught in the base path. Santana fires the ball to Lindor, who quickly throws to Ramírez, covering first base, and tags out García to complete the double play. What great awareness by Carlos Santana;

he knows he has García trapped and does not rush, and Lindor is quick to react to help finish the play. Matt Davidson bats now with two outs and the bases empty. The pitch by Carrasco and Davidson swings and launches another ball right at Santana, who steps on the base to retire the side. No strikeouts in this inning for Carrasco, who allows his first hit after retiring twelve straight batters to go along with seven strikeouts.

Chicago's first base runner doesn't last long as a ground ball double play sets down both Delmonico and García. It is now the eighth inning, and Gregory Infante, the White Sox reliever who replaced Reynaldo López in the seventh inning, stays out on the mound. The Indians have the lead by just a single run on a sacrifice fly by Naquin that came in the fourth. Edwin Encarnacion is batting; he is 1–3 with a single. Gregory Infante falls behind Edwin 3–1; the pitch is delivered, and ball four is called, as the pitch is high and wide. The Indians get their leadoff man on base; that is the third walk allowed by White Sox pitching today. Carlos Santana is up to bat now; he has made some big plays defensively in recent innings. He also has scored the only run in this game so far. White Sox reliever, Danny Farquhar, is called to take the mound, and he will pitch to Santana. Here comes his first pitch, "He drives this one high, he drives it deep to right this ball is gone! Over the bullpen into the seats in right field! Carlos Santana hits number twenty-three," Tom Hamilton comments.

A two-run blast by Carlos Santana gives the Tribe some separation; it is now a 3–0 lead in the top of the eighth! Yandy Díaz bats with the bases empty after the two-run home run by Santana. Díaz has already been walked one time in three plate appearances today. Three balls, no strikes, and Farquhar's pitch is too low for a called ball four, and Yandy Díaz takes first base. Greg Allen will run for Díaz with Almonte stepping up to bat. It is a three-run lead for the Indians in this eighth inning, still nobody out and a speedy Greg Allen running at first base. The pitch, Abe Almonte swings and shoots a base hit into center field! Greg Allen sprints to third, and the Indians have runners at the corners for Tyler Naquin, who drove home the team's first run in the fourth. Tito decides to substitute another pinch runner for the Indians; Bradley Zimmer will run for

Almonte at first base. The White Sox pitching is really struggling now as a third man is walked in this inning, the second free pass issued by Danny Farquhar. This inning started with a walk and a two-run home run by Carlos Santana. Five men have batted, and all five have reached, the bases are now full, and there's still nobody out.

Roberto Pérez is batting for a fourth time; he is 0–3, striking out twice already. The bases are loaded, and the pitch by Farquhar is delivered with the infield in. Perez's hit is grounded to Davidson at first, but he drops the ball again. Everybody is safe, and Matt Davidson's second error of the game costs his team a run as Greg Allen scores from third to make it 4–0 Tribe. A double play off the bat of Lindor and a strikeout by Lonnie Chisenhall ends the inning. Indians have bases full after the two-run homer but only add a single run. Four runs to nothing, the White Sox trail after seven and a half innings played in Chicago. Carlos Carrasco returns to the mound for the bottom of the eighth inning and is now pitching with a commanding four-run lead. Carrasco has retired nearly every batter he has faced. He has eight strikeouts and has only allowed two hits, one of them coming from the next man up, Avisaíl Garcia. It was García in the fifth inning that broke up Cookie's perfect game. Carrasco's pitch is swung on, and a shallow fly ball is lifted to Bradley Zimmer in center who makes the catch for the out. The left fielder Delmonico is now the batter; he is hitless with two groundouts in both at-bats. A 1–2 count on Delmonico as Carrasco is searching for his ninth strikeout in under eighty-five pitches. He delivers, Delmonico swings and misses as he can't catch up to the fastball!

Nine strikeouts have now been recorded for Carlos Carrasco; with two outs in the eighth, he has thrown just eighty-one pitches. Matt Davidson grounds out to Carlos Santana, and Carrasco retires the White Sox in order again for the sixth time in eight innings. The Indians will bat next with a 4–0 lead in the top of the ninth, and you can be sure Carrasco will try to convince Tito to let him go back to the mound to complete the shutout in the bottom half of the inning. The Indians score once more on a fielder's choice to take a 5–0 lead into the bottom of the ninth inning. José Ramírez comes home from second when the White Sox fail to turn an inning ending double play. Carrasco has pitched a gem to this point. Nine strikeouts on just two hits, and he is one out away from a complete game shutout. The center fielder, Adam Engel, is the batter, and the Indians need one more out to tie the team record for the longest winning streak in franchise history. The first pitch to Engel, he swings, and this ball jolts off the bat and carries to right center field and over the wall for a solo homer. Adam Engel has broken up the shutout on just the team's third hit. Alen Hanson will get another at-bat; he is 0–3 with two strikeouts. All three hits have come from three different batters.

"The 1–2 pitch swung on a dribbler rolled towards second. González gloves, throws, got 'em, ball game! The Indians make it fourteen straight! They equal the club record for the longest winning streak in franchise history. A record they set one year ago. And a chance to break it tomorrow night with arguably the best pitcher in the American League in Corey Kluber," Tom Hamilton comments.

Carlos Carrasco gets win number fourteen! He goes the distance and strikes out nine White Sox batters and allows just a single run that comes here in the ninth inning on a solo homer after he sets down the first two batters.

The Indians have won fourteen straight games with a chance to rewrite franchise history for the longest win streak if they can beat the White Sox in the series finale. Over these past two weeks, the Indians have outpitched and outscored their opponents, 98–26. The starting pitchers have been credited with twelve of the fourteen wins, and the run producers have hit more home runs than total runs allowed with twenty-eight. The Tribe has outscored their opponents by a grand total of seventy-two runs, and a win today would send them back to Cleveland with a sweep of the entire eleven-game road trip. Mike Pelfrey will pitch for the White Sox; he is three and ten on the season. Francisco Lindor will bat first for the Indians; he is just 2–11 in this series with one RBI that came in the first game. Mike Pelfrey fires strike one as Lindor lets it go by, and we are underway in Chicago.

The next pitch, Lindor drives this ball into the right center field gap that will be played by Engel off the wall. Lindor makes the turn at second, and he is headed for third and slides in safely as the throw is offline! Frankie Lindor with a leadoff triple to start this game, that is his third three bagger of the year, and the Indians are in business here early! Austin Jackson bats second, looking to drive home an early first inning run. With Lindor on third base, all the Tribe needs here is a medium deep fly ball or a groundout to score him. It is an even 1–1 count; Pelfrey's pitch to Jackson is delivered, and he swings and shoots a low line drive to center field where it falls and skips beyond Adam Engel. Jackson hustles to second base with the game's first RBI, and for the fifteenth straight game, the Indians score first! Yandy Díaz is now batting third, and the Indians have taken the early one-run lead and have nobody out.

Mike Pelfrey walks Díaz on six pitches; he threw the first two offerings for strikes but couldn't send Díaz back to the dugout. Instead, the Indians have two men on, and Encarnacion comes to the plate. Pelfrey fires a strike, and he gets ahead in the count, 0–1. "Two on nobody out and Edwin Encarnacion drives one to deep left field, back is Delmonico, it's gone to the bullpen! A four run first for Cleveland and were four batters into the game! Home run number thirty-three for Edwin and he's now driven home eighty-five on the year!" Matt Underwood exclaims. For the second straight start Corey Kluber will pitch with a 4–0 first inning lead.

The three-run bomb by Encarnacion is plenty when you have Corey Kluber as your starter. With a 4–0 Indians cushion, they do no more damage in the frame, and Chicago is coming to bat in the home half of the first. Yolmer Sánchez is the batter with his team in an early four-run hole. Kluber gets strike 1 as Sánchez fouls off the first pitch. Kluber delivers, and Yolmer Sánchez sends a deep drive to right field, and it will find the seats. A leadoff solo home run by the White Sox third baseman, and it is a 4–1 ball game in the bottom of the first. It is very uncommon to see Kluber give up a home run at such an early part of the game, and the Tribe lead is cut down to three. The second baseman, Yoán Moncada, is set down on three pitches. Austin Jackson fields the fly ball in left for the first out. José Abreu is batting third; he is not the designated hitter in this game but rather the first baseman.

We are still in the bottom of the first inning, the Indians with an early 4–1 lead. Kluber offers the 2–1 pitch to Abreu, and another ball is hammered to center field, and in an instant, what was a four nothing Cleveland lead is now down to two. Sánchez and now Abreu both take Kluber deep, and the Indians' lead has been cut in half. Three home runs in the first four outs—one by the Indians and two by the white Sox. Corey Kluber now faces Nicky Delmonico; he is playing in left and batting cleanup. Kluber gets ahead of Delmonico, no balls two strikes. Here's the pitch, swing and a miss! Delmonico chases the high fastball, and he can't get wood on it. That is the first strikeout of the game for Kluber, and Avisaíl García is the fifth batter this inning with two outs. Kluber is working with two strikes on García with the bases empty. The pitch by Kluber, swing and a miss by García! Well, a rather uncommon start for a pitcher who is likely to be nominated for the Cy Young award, but both home runs are solo, so his team still has a 4–2 lead after one inning. The Indians batted around in the first inning, so Lindor steps up for his second at bat. Francisco Lindor came home to score on the double by Austin Jackson after he led off the game with a triple. The pitcher Pelfrey has Lindor in an even count with the score 4–2 Indians at the start of this second inning. The pitch, Lindor drives this ball to deep right field and you can forget it! It is a slugfest here in Chicago!

Five tallies to two now, the Indians expand their lead on the solo blast by Francisco Lindor, and after just six outs, we have seen four home runs! Lindor came into this game on a cold streak, but he now has half of the cycle complete, and it is only the top of the second. Edwin Encarnacion, who hit the three-run home run in the first inning that gave the Indians a 4-0 lead, reaches base with a two-out walk. Carlos Santana gets his second at-bat; he started this game with a groundout to Abreu at first base. Mike Pelfrey sends his pitch, and Santana lofts a shallow flyball to Adam Engel in center field, who catches it for the third out. The Indians have added a fifth run with Lindor's twenty-seventh homer on the year, and the Tribe advantage is now three going to the bottom of the second inning.

Matt Davidson is Chicago's designated hitter and is batting for the first time in this final game. The White Sox know all too well that despite the two home run balls that they hit in the first inning, Kluber remains calm and focused, especially with a lead. Davidson in a two-strike hole, the pitch, swing, and a miss! Kluber gets Davidson to chase a high fastball for his third strikeout and the first out. Omar Narváez bats; he was catcher for the White Sox in game 1, but in games 2 and 3, it is Brantly and Smith. It is a good hitter's count, now 3–1 on Narváez. Kluber delivers, and this ball is swung on and chopped right at Lindor, who quickly throws to Santana for the second out.

The shortstop, Tyler Saladino, is batting with the bases empty, and there are two outs in the second. The first pitch by Kluber is a fastball for strike 1 as Saladino swings and misses. It is now an even 2–2 count. Kluber delivers his pitch, and Saladino unloads but misses! Kluber gets him to chase the pitch in the dirt, and it is a good second inning recovery by Kluber. The Tribe's ace adds two more strikeouts, so give him four on the day; he is pitching with a three-run lead. Lonnie Chisenhall bats first in the top of the third inning, and he singled in his first at-bat but did not score. Chisenhall is behind Mike Pelfrey, 1–2, the pitch, and he swings through the ninety-seven-mile-per-hour heater. One out and Yan Gomes will step in; he is 1–1 for the day. Mike Pelfrey delivers, and Gomes swings and finds a gap in center field. The ball gets by Engel and rolls to the wall for a double. Yan Gomes is now 2–2 in the game, and that is his fifteenth double on the season. Bradley Zimmer is the next out, and for the second time today, he goes down on strikes, once swinging and now looking as Pelfrey's slider just catches the inside corner of the plate. Erik González bats with two outs and Yan Gomes, standing on second base. González was the final out of the four-run first inning. It is now a 5–2 Tribe lead.

"Now the 2–2 pitch, swung on blasted deep left field this ball gone! Erik González with his third home run!" Tom Hamilton announces.

The Indians with home run number 3 today take a 7–2 lead, their largest lead of the game! It is at-bats from players like González's utility players whose names you may not hear too often, but González, Díaz, and Urshela show that everybody has played a part in this streak! Frankie Lindor is retired for the third out, on a groundout, and for the first time today, he doesn't get a hit. Lindor is now two for three, but he has scored twice. Kluber strolls back to the mound to pitch the bottom of the third with a comfortable lead. Adam Engle takes his first swings in this ball game; he is facing one of the most dominant pitchers in the American League. Kluber, working ahead once again, has a 1–2 count looking for another strikeout. The pitch, high and inside, and Engel has to back away. A ninety-six-mile-per-hour heater from Kluber evens the count, two balls, two strikes. Gomes gives his pitcher the sign, and Kluber's 2–2 pitch is swung on and missed! Adam Engel chases a pitch several feet in front of home plate. The ball must have slipped out of his hands but gives Corey Kluber five strikeouts.

Yolmer Sánchez bats for a second time; he led off the bottom of the first inning with the solo home run that at the time made the score 4–1 Cleveland. Sánchez works the count full; he has seen seven pitches in this at-bat, fouling away the last two from Kluber. The payoff pitch is delivered and strike three called! Sánchez looks at the changeup just above the knees and give Kluber six strikeouts on the day. After allowing the two home runs in the first inning, he has struck out two batters in each of the last three innings. Yoán Moncada lines out to Erik González for the third out, and Corey Kluber has set down eight straight White Sox since Abreu's solo blast in the first inning. It is the top of the seventh inning in the Windy City with the Indians now facing Chris Beck, who took over the mound duties in the fifth inning. With a 7–2 count, the Indians are leading; they last scored in the third inning.

The White Sox have not scored since the first inning. There is one out for Bradley Zimmer as Gomes strikes out swinging to begin the inning. So far Zimmer is hitless in three at-bats with two strikeouts. On the first pitch, Zimmer swings and smokes a deep drive that carries just over the head of Engel to the wall in center field, and Zimmer gallops to third as Adam Engle does not play it off the wall well; it will be recorded as a double and an error. Erik González bats with one out and a runner on third base. He hit the two-run home run in the third inning that made the score 7–2, and that's where we stand now. Chris Beck is behind in the count, 2–1, trying to keep any more runs from being added to the deficit. The two one pitch, Erik González sends a flyball to left field, but Delmonico is there to catch it. Bradley Zimmer tags up and sprints home, trying to score as the throw home is not nearly in time and the Indians' lead is now 8–2.

There are two outs now, and before Lindor bats, the White Sox bring on Jace Fry to pitch. Lindor has tripled and homered and is batting now with the bases empty; his team has just added a run, and they now lead by six. Lindor has fallen behind Fry 0–2 and awaits the pitch. Here it comes, Lindor swings and hits a sharp single into center field for his third hit; he is just a double shy of the cycle! Greg Allen gets his first at-bat of this ball game, he replaced Austin Jackson in left field in the sixth inning. Jace Fry's first pitch and it gets to the backstop as it sails over the catcher's head as Lindor moves up to second base. The score is 8–2, and the Tribe has two outs in the top of the seventh inning in game four of this series in Chicago. Greg Allen works the count to 3–1, a good hitter's count.

"The pitch, Allen with a drive, to deep left awaaaaay back and gone! How about that! The first major league home run for Greg Allen! Oh, did he put a charge into that one. It's 10–2 Indians, oh, is this kid going to be something special! Thank you, Jonathan Lucroy!" Tom Hamilton comments.

Home run number 4 in this ball game for the Indians, and it is officially a rout! The Indians are well in charge of this ball game, just nine outs away from winning their fifteenth straight game! The White Sox strand a base runner at second as Omar Narváez lines out to Lindor for the last out of the seventh inning. Corey Kluber has no strikeouts this inning, but he has blown away thirteen in seven innings of work. Corey Kluber has pitched another gem, and it looks like he will not return after this inning. Talk about making a strong recovery, the Indians' ace allows two home runs in the first inning that brought the Sox within two runs and then allows only one more hit for the game for a total of three, wow! It is the top of the ninth inning, and Cleveland is leading Chicago by a score of 10–2. The Indians have had the lead the entire game, but at one point, the score was 4–2. Bradley

Zimmer leads off the ninth; he doubled and scored in the seventh inning on a sacrifice fly hit by González. The pitch, Zimmer sends a fly ball to right but not deep, and Liriano grabs it for the first out.

Erik González is the batter, and he has three RBIs with a homer and a sac fly. The 1–0 pitch and González drives this ball deep toward the wall in center. Engel races back to the wall—it is gone! Erik González has hit the Indians' fifth home run, and he has his first multihomer game of his career. At 11–2, the Indians have been dominating the White Sox all game long. Lindor and Allen are both set down to end the top of the ninth, and the Indians lead in this game by nine. Craig Breslow pitches the bottom of the ninth, and the Indians are three outs from winning their fifteenth consecutive ball game, including every game on this eleven-game road trip. Yoán Moncada leads off; he is 0–3 with a strikeout, but this is the first time he is facing someone other than Corey Kluber. Moncada reaches base with a five-pitch walk to start the bottom of the ninth. José Abreu steps in; he hit the second home run for the White Sox back in the first inning, but they haven't scored since then. Abreu gets down in the count 0–2, here comes the pitch, a swing, and the ball is grounded right at Lindor, who flips the ball to González, who then fires the ball over to first base for the double play!

The White Sox are down by nine, and Nicky Delmonico could be the last man for Craig Breslow to face. Breslow has Delmonico down, 1–2, and is just one strike away from finishing a game that would rewrite Indians' history. In 2016, the Tribe won fourteen straight games before they lost to the Toronto Blue Jays.

"The pitch, strike three called ball game and Cleveland Indians history! For the first time in the long history of the Cleveland Indians, they have a fifteen-game winning streak! The longest in baseball in fifteen years and they decided it early tonight routing the Chicago White Sox by a final score of 11–2!" Tom Hamilton declares.

Another dominant performance for Corey Kluber, who pitches seven innings and strikes out a baker's dozen! Corey Kluber is now 15–4 with an ERA just above 2.50. The Indians started this winning streak at home but haven't played at Progressive Field since they faced and beat the Royals on August 27. It is now September 7, and the Indians, after winning eleven games on the road, return home to play the Baltimore Orioles.

Chapter 5

---※❯❯❯ ❰❰❰※---

Home Sweep Home, Games 16–18

Today continues a new era in Cleveland Indians baseball, as they are the owners of the longest winning streak in the American League in fifteen years since the Oakland A's won twenty straight games in 2002. The Cleveland Indians started a four-game win streak in Cleveland before they took it on the road battling and wining all eleven road games in New York, Detroit, and Chicago. The Tribe now starts a ten-game homestand beginning with a weekend series against the Baltimore Orioles. Mike Clevinger will be the starter for the Indians; his last start was in Detroit on September 1. It was the second game of the doubleheader and he allowed zero runs in six innings. Clevinger begins the contest by facing Tim Beckham, who takes strike 1, and we are underway at the corner of Carnegie and Ontario.

The next pitch and Beckham swings and sends a sharp drive right at Jay Bruce, who snares the ball for the first out. Manny Machado bats in the second spot with one out in the top of the first inning. The 0–2 pitch, Machado swings and hits this ball into shallow center field; Austin Jackson runs in and grabs it for the second out. The second baseman, Jonathan Schoop, steps in and takes a strike from Clevinger. No balls one strike, and the next pitch is hit to deep right field but foul, and Schoop falls behind 0–2. The pitch, Schoop swings and grounds this ball to third Yandy Díaz, who nestles it in his glove and fires the ball to Santana for a one-two-three first inning for Mike Clevinger. No runs for the Orioles, and the Indians will take their first swings with Lindor leading off. Francisco Lindor and the Indians will face Wade Miley in game one of this weekend series. Miley quickly falls behind, 2–1, Lindor, who yanks the last pitch foul. Miley's next two pitches are ruled a ball, and Lindor reaches base with a leadoff walk. Austin Jackson is the batter, and on the first pitch, he hits a ground ball sharply at Jonathan Schoop, who turns and retires Lindor at second for the force, and there is one out with Jackson on first.

Yandy Díaz is third in today's lineup, and he is quickly down in a two-strike hole. The 0–2 pitch, he swings and rips this ball far to right field for a single; Jackson moves to second, and Edwin Encarnacion steps into the batter's box with two men on base. Wade Miley fires strike 1 past Edwin, who is looking to make something happen with two runners on. For the past fifteen games, the Indians have scored first and have never looked back. Only twice have they fallen behind on the scoreboard after they have taken the lead. The 0–1 pitch to Encarnacion, he swings and this ball is hammered to deep center field, and Adam Jones will watch it sail over the wall! Edwin Encarnacion gives the parrot a ride! For sixteen games in a row, the Tribe has taken the first lead in a game. It is 3–0 Cleveland on Encarnacion's thirty-fourth bomb of the year that finds the trees in deep center field, and the crowd is on their feet at Progressive Field. Over thirty thousand fans have come out today, and they are ecstatic to see their team back home.

Jay Bruce is the batter; he has been riding the bench for a while now, and he is batting with two strikes. The 1–2 pitch, it is a swing and a miss by Bruce, and there are two outs now. Brandon Guyer strikes out chasing a breaking ball, and the inning is over. But it is a three-run first inning for the Tribe, thanks to the blast to center field by Encarnacion. Trey Mancini is batting for the first time with a man on first. Mike Clevinger walks Adam Jones on four straight pitches to begin the top of the second inning. Clevinger has fallen behind, 2–0, and he has tossed six straight balls and is struggling with his command. The next pitch, a swing, and Mancini grounds a ball third base side, Yandy Díaz makes a quick throw to González to get Jones and then the relay to get Mancini, and they turn two. Another walk is given up by Clevinger, but Mark Trumbo on a 0–1 pitch hits a ball on the ground to Carlos Santana for the third out. Clevinger has issues finding the strike zone, but a double play helps eliminate the O's scoring chance. We've played one and a half innings, and the Indians are in front with a 3–0 lead.

A double play is said to be a pitcher's best friend, and in the bottom of the second inning, Wade Miley escapes a jam as Frankie Lindor grounds into a six-four-three double play started by Tim Beckham and finished off by Jonathan Schoop. The score remains 3–0 Indians after two innings. Right fielder Seth Smith will face Mike Clevinger for the first time tonight. The pitch and the ball is chopped foul back behind home plate for strike 1. On an even count, Smith fouls off another ball, and the count stays at 2–2 on Seth Smith. Clevinger delivers his next pitch, and it is a swing and a miss by Smith! A fastball that is right down the middle, but he blows it by the right fielder for strikeout number 1! Caleb Joseph steps to the plate, and Clevinger quickly gets ahead with no balls and two strikes as both pitches are fouled into the stands. Clevinger's 0–2 pitch, strike 3 is called! Two strikeouts in a row for Mike Clevinger, and he is cruising in this inning. Mike Clevinger's third walk and a base hit by Machado bringings Jonathan Schoop to the plate; the Orioles are down three runs and could use a big hit with two outs. Clevinger's first pitch is too low, and Schoop gets ahead in the count. It is now an even 2–2 count on Schoop as he and his team are down three runs, but one swing could tie this game. Two men on base and here's the pitch…it is a swing and a miss! The ball breaks away from the batter, and he swings over the top of it.

Clevinger gets into some two-out trouble after striking out Smith and Joseph but gets the job done himself with three erasers to strike out the side in the top of the third. Yandy Díaz is the Tribe's leadoff batter now in the bottom of the sixth inning with the Indians still leading 3–0. Díaz is 1–2 today with a single and a run scored. Wade Miley has Díaz down 0–2, searching for strikeout number five in the game. The two-strike pitch to Díaz, he swings, and this ball is headed to left field and will get beyond Trey Mancini for a leadoff double as Díaz has his second hit. Carlos Santana now bats after Encarnacion and Jay Bruce came up empty, both hitting into groundouts to Chris Davis at first base. Yandy Díaz is the base runner at third, and it is a 1–1 count on Santana. Miley's pitch and Santana sends a drive to medium deep right field…this ball is falling and it hits the chalk and bounces over the sidewall for a ground-rule double. Díaz comes home to score, and Carlos Santana's thirty-third double of the year gives Cleveland a 4–0 advantage. What a clutch piece of two out hitting by Santana to give the Indians some insurance. In a pitching change for the Orioles, Miguel Castro replaces Wade Miley, who surrenders four runs in five and two-thirds innings pitched.

It is now the top of the seventh inning, and the Birds are behind the Indians by four runs, and Tyler Olson will be the new Indians' pitcher coming on to take over for Mike Clevinger, who strikes out seven in six innings of work. Olson makes quick work of the Orioles, give him one strikeout as he fans Mark Trumbo. That is the second time Trumbo has struck out in three at bats; he is 0–3 on the day. Often during this streak, we have credited the starting pitching and the offense, but the bullpen has been a big part of the winning as witnessed by the three-up, three-down inning from Tyler Olson. A team can't be in position to win sixteen straight games without a fantastic bullpen. In the bottom half of the seventh inning in Cleveland, Miguel Castro stays in the game, as so far he has only pitched one-third of the sixth inning. Francisco Lindor is the batter after Erik González grounded out to the shortstop, Tim Beckham. Lindor is 1–2 in today's contest with a double. The pitch by Castro and Lindor singles a ground ball into right field, and now he has two hits on the day.

With the bases loaded for the Indians, Bradley Zimmer is walked intentionally, and Giovanny Urshela reaches base on a walk after Miguel Castro had him down with two strikes. Edwin Encarnacion has gone hitless since he smoked the three-run home run in the first. Now he gets fanned on five pitches, and the bases stay loaded for Jay Bruce with two outs. Bruce is behind in the count 0–2 with the bases loaded, and Frankie Lindor is the runner at third base. The pitch, down in the dirt but O's catcher, Caleb Joseph, can't find the baseball. Lindor sprints and slides in safely to make the score 5–0 Indians. What hustle by Lindor, you can take that risk with a 4–0 lead, and it paid off.

As we move to the top of the ninth inning, the Indians have a comfortable five-run lead as Nick Goody is trying to nail down the team's sixteenth straight win. The Orioles get a two-out single from Trey Mancini, but the Indians have nobody warming up, so it is up to Goody. Chris Davis is the last hope for Baltimore to keep this game alive for his team. Goody's pitch, and with a swing and a miss, he gets ahead, 0–1. Davis takes Goody's next pitch high and wide to even the count. The 1–1 pitch from Nick Goody…it is a swing and a ball hit into the shift; Lindor gloves, throws, and gets him! Sixteen consecutive wins for the Cleveland Indians! They blank the Birds, 5–0, to begin this three-game series as the Tribe started the scoring early with the big three-run home run by Edwin Encarnacion in the bottom of the first inning. Mike Clevinger earns win number 9 as he strikes out seven batters in six innings. Wade Miley takes his twelfth loss with an ERA now just below five at 4.96. The Indians have returned home after sweeping the eleven-game road trip, and they continue this improbable win streak. The Indians reduce their magic number for the division title down to eleven as they are in search of a second straight division crown.

From Progressive Field in Downtown Cleveland, Ohio, a near sellout crowded of over thirty thousand fans continue to file in on this beautiful Saturday afternoon in September. The hometown fans have come to see what they hope will be the Indians' seventeenth consecutive win, a new club record with every victory. The Indians took game 1 yesterday by a convincing score of 5–0. The win also reduced their magic number to eleven. Josh Tomlin makes his second start since his return from the disabled list on September 3 when he pitched and notched the win in Detroit. Tomlin's first pitch is too low, and we are underway at the corner of Carnegie and Ontario. The leadoff man for Baltimore, Tim Beckham, swings at the second pitch and sends a ball to center field, not deep, and Bradley Zimmer grabs it for out number 1. Josh Tomlin is now facing Manny

Machado, who swings at the 0–1 pitch and hits a single by the diving Giovanny Urshela for the Orioles' first hit. Jonathan Schoop bats in the third spot; he works the count full after Tomlin fires the first two pitches in for strikes. Tomlin often avoids the walk, and more often than not, he will retire his man.

The payoff pitch and Schoop hits a fly ball to right field where Jay Bruce calls for it and makes the grab; there are two outs as he squeezes the ball in his glove. The center fielder, Adam Jones, swings and slaps a single into center field. Machado is held up at third on the throw by Zimmer, and Baltimore is threatening to snap Cleveland's mark in which they have scored first in every game in their long-winning streak. Trey Mancini is the left fielder batting with runners at the corners and two outs with a chance to score first against this prodigious pitching staff. Tomlin's 1–2 pitch to Mancini is swung on, grounded sharply to Lindor, who throws but not quite in time to throw out the runner, and Manny Machado scores to give the Orioles a 1–0 lead here in the first inning. That is the first run the Indians have allowed at home in thirty-seven innings.

With O's on first and second for Chris Davis, Tomlin is trying to strand these runners, as he has two strikes on Davis. The 1–2 pitch, a swing and a miss by Chris Davis! Well, the streak in which the Tribe scores first is over, but they have nine innings to erase a one-run deficit. As we go to the bottom of the third inning in Cleveland the Orioles have a 1–0 lead over the Indians, Baltimore's starter, Gabriel Ynoa, has retired the first six batters he has faced. Bradley Zimmer bats for the first time and sends a fly ball to the center fielder, Adam Jones, to lead off the inning for Cleveland. Yan Gomes, the catcher, steps in and takes his first swings in hopes of getting something started for the Tribe. Gomes steps in with an even 2–2 count and swings and shoots a single over third base for the team's first hit; he is also the first base runner.

Giovanny Urshela is the next batter and takes strike 1 from Ynoa to fall behind in the count, 0–1. The next pitch is offered, and he swings and smokes the ball foul and into the seats to fall into an 0–2 hole. Gabriel Ynoa is about to make his 0–2 pitch to Gio Urshela.

"Here it comes, a swing and a high drive, deep center field this ball off the top of the nineteen-foot wall, game will be tied Gomes is scoring Urshela in with a double! Oh, did he put a charge into that one," Tom Hamilton comments.

This game is tied one run apiece; the Indians' breakthrough in the bottom of the third inning, and it is a brand-new ball game, thanks to Urshelas's RBI double! Lindor and Chisenhall go down on a flyout and a groundout to take us to the top of the fourth inning; the score is even at one in Cleveland. Adam Jones leads off the top of the inning for the Birds; he is 1–1 with a single. Tomlin sends his first pitch, and Jones hits a ball sharply to second. Urshela scoops the ball up, and he throws the runner out to begin the fourth. Trey Mancini bats with one out, and he singled home a run on an infield hit in the top of the first inning. Tomlin moves ahead in the count and has two strikes on Mancini; he is working quickly. The 0–2 pitch and strike 3 is called on Mancini, and he can't believe it. Tomlin places a curveball upstairs in a dangerous zone, but the umpire says, "Nope, that's a strike." Mancini has some words for the umpire before he walks away. Chris Davis gets his second at-bat he struck out his first time up. Tomlin falls behind, 3–0, on Davis, and he wants to make a perfect pitch to climb back into the count. Here it comes, there's a strike, and the count is 3–1.

Tomlin's next pitch is delivered, and Davis chops a slow ground ball right at Lindor, who throws to Carlos Santana for the third out. Ten batters in a row have now been set down by Josh Tomlin. The Indians come to bat in the bottom of the fourth and will try to take their first lead. Carlos Santana leads off for the Indians; he grounded out his first time up. Ynoa's payoff pitch and Santana swings and shoots a ball into the right field corner. Santana rounds first and slides safely into second for his thirty-fourth double. Edwin Encarnacion is now batting; he is 0–1 so far today with a fly out. Edwin swings and connects on the 1–1 pitch, and first baseman Chris Davis will take it himself for the out. Santana moves ninety feet closer to home up to third base. Jay Bruce, the right fielder that the Indians acquired earlier in the year, is looking to drive home Santana from third with one out in the fourth inning. Gabriel Ynoa's pitch is taken for a ball Ynoa falls behind, 1–0.

"Here's the 1–0, swung on line drive base hit into right field, and that will put the Indians in front two to one on the RBI single by Jay Bruce," declares Jim Rosenhaus.

The Indians get another base hit from Yandy Díaz but strand both men on base, and the score stays at 2–1. Bradley Zimmer strikes out, and Yan Gomes flies out to Adam Jones in center field. Mark Trumbo is the leadoff batter for Baltimore in the fifth; he previously lined out to Jay Bruce to start the second inning. Trumbo takes strike one from Josh Tomlin, who has made some great pitches since the last out of the first inning. With two balls and one strike, Tomlin's pitch is foul tipped at home to even the count at 2–2. Tomlin's next pitch to Trumbo is swung on and missed! A cut fastball with great movement moving away from the hitter, and Tomlin records his third strikeout of this game. The Orioles' next two batters don't reach base, and Josh Tomlin has set down thirteen straight opponents, eight of them have grounded out. There are two quick outs for Gabriel Ynoa to start the bottom of the fifth inning. Urshela and Lindor make solid contact but can't find a gap in the outfield. Lonnie Chisenhall bats third in the inning; he is hitless to this point. Chisenhall gets ahead in the count, and he swings at the third pitch and lines a single into center field to keep the inning alive.

Carlos Santana steps in; he scored the go-ahead run for the Tribe in the bottom of the fourth. The score remains 2–1, and the Indians have the lead with two outs and Chisenhall on first base. The 2–2 pitch and Santana smokes this ball deep to left field; it hits off the wall above Mancini, and Chisenhall comes home from first base to make it 3–1 Tribe! A two out double off the wall in left field for Carlos Santana as he records his second double of the game, and the Indians are looking to pull farther ahead. Pitcher Mychal Givens replaces Gabriel Ynoa with two outs after the RBI double by Santana; he will face Edwin Encarnacion. On Givens' first pitch, he gets Encarnacion to ground out to the shortstop, Tim Beckham, but the Indians increase their lead by a run, and now Cleveland leads Baltimore, 3–1, after five complete innings.

As we move to the top of the sixth inning, Josh Tomlin will remain in the game, and he is pitching with a two-run lead. Tim Beckham is the leadoff man in the lineup for Baltimore and will bat searching for his first hit of the day. Tomlin's first pitch is outside for a ball; he has set down thirteen straight batters and is throwing a whale of a game. Tomlin's next pitch is offered, and Beckham swings and drives a ball deep to left; it is a souvenir over the nineteen-foot wall for a leadoff home run. The lead is cut down to one, 3–2 Indians with no outs in the top of the sixth. Tito decides that will be all for Josh Tomlin; Joe Smith will come in the game and try and preserve this slim lead. Tomlin is still in position to get his ninth win, but it will be up to the bullpen now. Reliever Joe Smith strikes out both Schoop and Mancini after giving up a base hit, but the Indians keep the lead, 3–2, now heading to the bottom of the seventh inning.

A new pitcher for the Orioles is set to start the bottom of the seventh inning, as Darren O'Day will take over as the second relief pitcher. Giovanny Urshela bats he doubled home a run off the wall in left that started the scoring for the Indians back in the bottom of the third inning. Urshela faces O'Day with two strikes and swings through a breaking ball, and he is out number one. The Indians still lead, 3–2, in the bottom of the seventh with Lindor batting a fourth time while seeking his first hit. With two strikes on Lindor, O'Day fires and Lindor yanks a ball deep to right field, and down the line it goes and gone! Francisco Lindor with his twenty-eighth home run of the year makes it a 4–2 Tribe lead here in the seventh inning. The Indians move back up by two, and the crowd is roaring here in Downtown Cleveland. We move to the top of the ninth inning, and a crowd of 30,459 is up on their feet at The Corner of Carnegie and Ontario! Cody Allen is one strike away from his twenty-fifth save and, more importantly, continuing this incredible streak.

"The 0–2 pitch, a swing and a miss, ball game, they've done it again! Seventeen in a-row! The Indians historical streak marches on! 4–2 the Indians wipe out the Orioles today. A winning streak that started on August 24, it will continue at least until September 10," Tom Hamilton says.

This weekend series between the Indians and the Orioles wraps up today, and the Indians are looking to continue a winning streak that began on August 24 when they beat the Boston Red Sox by a score of 13–6. The Tribe has won seventeen consecutive games, the fourth longest win streak in Major League Baseball since the Oakland Athletics were victorious with twenty in a row in 2002. Trevor Bauer will get the start in this third game of the series; his last appearance came in Chicago on September 4 where he recorded the win pitching six and one-third innings. Tim Beckham will lead off this game; the shortstop has only one hit in seven at-bats this series. Bauer makes the first pitch, and swinging right away, Beckham grounds a ball to Lindor, who gloves and throws him out to begin this game. Manny Machado steps in as the next batter; there is one out in the top of the first inning. Trevor Bauer fires strike one past Machado. Bauer has become one of the top pitchers in the American League, and he plays a big role in this Indians' rotation. Machado swings, and the ball deflects off Bauer's leg, and José Ramírez has no play, and it is an infield base hit. The Orioles have a base runner and a good first scoring chance in the inning with Adam Jones stepping up to the plate.

Yesterday in game two of the series, the Orioles scored first, but it didn't matter, as the Tribe was victorious. It was the first time during this win streak that the Indians did not take the first lead, but the Orioles couldn't make it stand up. Now there is a full count on Adam Jones as he is trying to get some scoring started for his team with one out; he does not want to blow this opportunity. The pitch by Bauer, a swing, and the ball is grounded to Ramírez at second, who flips it to Lindor, who then throws to Santana, and the Indians turn an inning ending four-six-three double play! Trevor Bauer escapes the first inning jam he was in but tosses twenty pitches. The Indians will bat next on this cloudless night, and we are scoreless in Cleveland. Francisco Lindor leads off for the Indians; he was involved in turning the inning ending double play. Jeremy Hellickson is the starting hurler for the O's; he is 8–8 on the season with an ERA above four. The first pitch is delivered, and Lindor swings and drives a ball to left field as it bangs off the wall; Lindor sprints to second base with a stand-up double.

Lonnie Chisenhall is the batter now; he has been the Indians' left fielder for the past few games. He is normally in right, but nevertheless, it hasn't hurt the team defensively. Chisenhall takes a strike as he falls behind 0–1. Hellickson looks at second and is keeping an eye on Lindor; one wouldn't expect him to try and swipe third as he is already in scoring position. The 1–1 pitch and Chisenhall sends a shallow fly ball toward short, and it is going to fall in shallow center over the head of Tim Beckham, and Lindor alertly hustles to third. There are now runners on first and third for José Ramírez; he is the American League leader in extra base hits with forty-seven, and it is a good scoring chance for the Tribe. On the first pitch, Ramírez hits a slow-bouncing ball to Schoop, who needs to run in to snare it and makes the toss to first to complete the play. The out will score Lindor from third, and the Indians take an early 1–0 lead.

The Indians again score first as they have done it in all but one game during this streak when they gave up the first run in yesterday's ball game. Encarnacion and Bruce do not reach base, and the Indians strand a runner at second but take a 1–0 lead. One inning is complete in Cleveland, and it is Trevor Bauer back to the mound where he will look to keep this one-run lead. Trey Mancini will grab a bat and lead off for the Birds in the top of the second inning. Mancini doesn't offer at the first pitch from Bauer, and he gets ahead in the count. The 1–0 pitch is below the batter's knees, and Bauer has fallen behind Mancini, two balls and no strikes. The next pitch is offered, and Trey Mancini hits a slow ground ball to Yandy Díaz at third, who gloves it and throws him out to start the inning. Chris Davis will bat with one out after Mancini grounds out to Díaz at the hot corner. Baer's pitch is a fastball swung over the top for strike one. Bauer is now ahead, 0–2, and here comes the pitch, Davis swings and lines a ball to left, and backpaddling is Chisenhall for the catch, and there are two gone. Mark Trumbo hits a sharp ground ball at Ramírez, and he fires the ball to Santana to end the inning, and the Orioles go one-two-three for the first time today.

Another strong inning from Bauer, while only the second inning, but the stakes are high for his team. As we go to the bottom of the second inning, Jeremy Hellickson puts up a zero as Santana,

Díaz, and Zimmer all fly out, and the score stays at 1–0 Cleveland. In the top of the third inning, the Orioles trail, 1–0, and Bauer is coming off a three-up, three-down inning. The Oriole's catcher, Welington Castillo, leads off, and his team is down by a run. Castillo falls behind, 0–1; Bauer's second pitch is fouled off at home plate that brings us to 0–2. The pitch to Castillo and strike three called! That is the first strikeout for Trevor Bauer today as he gets the Orioles' catcher looking at a curveball. Now up for his first at-bat is Seth Smith; the right fielder sends a fly ball right at Jay Bruce, who catches it for the second out. The O's lineup flips back to the leadoff man, Tim Beckham; he is batting with two outs and nobody on base, as Bauer is looking for another quick inning. The pitch and Beckham sends a deep drive to right field. It bounces in front of the warning track and launches above the wall for a ground rule double. Give Tim Beckham his sixteenth double, and the Orioles will look to even this game up at one.

The third baseman, Manny Machado, is batting with the potential tying run on base, and he needs a two-out hit to score the runner from second base. Machado falls behind, 0–1, the next pitch from Bauer, and he swings and rips this ball far but foul into the seats. If that ball stays fair, the Orioles grab a 2–1 lead. Bauer checks the runner as he makes his two-strike pitch, and it is a swing and a miss! Machado is blown away on the breaking pitch. Bauer has said how much he has worked on his breaking pitch when he warms up, and it gives the Tribe pitcher his second strikeout. As we move to the top of the sixth inning, Baltimore ties this game at one on a one out double by Manny Machado. Then Jonathan Schoop singles him home on a ball that he hits to left, Chisenhall has no play. The side is retired when Bauer and the Indians record their second double play, and the Indians will look to recover and retake the lead in the bottom of the sixth. Roberto Pérez leads off for the Indians; he grounded out to the pitcher his first time up. It is a tie ball game in the bottom of the sixth inning, and the Indians catcher is looking to start this inning off on a positive note for the Tribe.

"He delivers, Pérez with a drive, deep left field, it is gone! Roberto Pérez hits number five, and the Indians have a 2–1 lead here in inning number six," Tom Hamilton comments.

Frankie Lindor steps up to bat as his team has just regained the lead on the solo blast to left field by Roberto Pérez. The first pitch is offered to Lindor as he swings and slices his bat in two. Lindor now works the count full; Jeremy Hellickson has made seven pitches to the Indians All-Star shortstop.

"The payoff pitch swung on liner deep right field down the line it goes foul and Lindor has broken another bat. This will be his third bat of the at bat. Now the pitch to him, a swing and a drive, to deep right awwaay back gone! Back-to-back jacks! Pérez and now Lindor," Tom Hamilton adds.

As soon as he swings, Lindor looks over to the dugout with a huge smile. He rides the bases home, and when he gets back to the dugout, he is given the bat by Abraham Almonte. The Indians respond with two solo home runs. They go back to back and now lead the Orioles, 3–1! It is the top of the seventh inning, and Trevor Bauer is now working with a two-run lead after the Indians homer twice in the sixth. Trey Mancini bats; he was a strikeout victim in the fourth inning. Bauer has allowed six hits, and he has struck out seven batters. The pitch and Mancini grounds this one to Lindor, who plays it beautifully, and throws a dart to first. One out in the seventh inning and eight outs away from continuing this phenomenal streak as a win today for the Tribe will give them eighteen consecutive wins. First baseman, Chris Davis, is the next batter; he also was fanned by Trevor Bauer to end the fourth inning for the Orioles. Bauer makes his pitch, and Davis sends this ball deep to left down the line, and it reaches the seats in fair territory. Chris Davis has an opposite field home run that he kept fair to bring the Birds a run closer at 3–2 Cleveland. That is all for Bauer; Terry Francona has seen enough and will bring on Joe Smith.

For the second start in a row, Bauer goes six and one-third innings; he is now in position to win his sixteenth game. Joe Smith sets down Mark Trumbo and Welington Castillo, but the Cleveland Indians' lead is reduced to a single run. As we go to the top of the ninth inning at Progressive Field, Cody Allen, the closer, will try to slam the door on the Orioles. Allen pitches well facing the first two opponents; it is 3–2 Tribe with one out to go. Allen strikes out Schoop and Jones to make quick work of the first two batters. The Orioles are down to their final out, and Trey Mancini, who is hitless so far, will try to keep his team's hopes alive.

"Allen into the motion, here it comes, swung on looping liner to right coming on Jay Bruce makes the catch, ball game! Right now, there is no stopping the Cleveland Indians. They sweep the Baltimore Orioles. More importantly, history continues to march on! Eighteen in a row for the Cleveland Indians, a franchise record, and for the Indians, this is just the fifth time in Major League Baseball history we have eighteen wins in a row!" Tom Hamilton declares.

Trevor Bauer gets his sixteenth win on the season, and he is asked in the clubhouse about his thoughts on his team's winning streak. "We're playing the type of baseball that we knew we could from the beginning. We know we have the talent to do stuff like this and to win a high percentage of our games. We're playing with the right intensity, we're playing with the right focus, the right energy level. It's been a lot of fun. If you look at the last two months of us playing, I think that's more like what we know we can do," Trevor Bauer remarks.

Mike Clevinger Pitches the Tribe to Another Win; Photo by Keith Allison

Carlos Santana's Home Run, Tribe Scores First for
12th Straight Game; Photo by Keith Allison

Lindor and Jackson Celebrate the Indian's 17th
Straight Win; Photo by Keith Allison

Jay Bruce's Game Winning Single Sets New Major League Baseball
Win Streak Record at 22 Wins; Photo by Keith Allison

Corey Kluber Complete Game Shutout Ties A.L. Win
Streak Record at 20 Wins; Photo by apardavila

Meeting the "Voice of the Cleveland Indians", Tom Hamilton
with my brother Matt Brigeman, June 20, 2016

Chapter 6

———⟫⟫⟩ ⟨⟨⟨———

American League History Made, Games 19–21

Ten days ago, on September 1, the Indians were in Detroit playing the Tigers and trying to win their eighth straight game. Now we flip the scenery to Progressive Field in Cleveland where the Indians will be playing for their nineteenth win in a row. They swept the four-game series at Comerica Park, including a day/night doubleheader in games one and two. The Cleveland Indians, after yesterday's victory, which completed a three-game sweep verses the Orioles, have now claimed the best record in the American League with a one-game lead over the Houston Astros. The Tribe's record is an impressive 87–56, thirty-one games above .500! Throughout this incredible streak, the Indians players have done an amazing job of taking care of the task at hand. When asked about the streak, players in the clubhouse say that they throw all the previous wins aside and that they don't look toward what could happen but only at the current task at hand. They play pitch by pitch, out by out every single game, and that is music to Tito's ears!

For this next game, Carlos Carrasco will take the mound for the Indians searching for his fifteenth win of the season. The second baseman, Ian Kinsler, leads off for the Tigers and takes strike one to begin this ball game. Carrasco falls to a full count now after Kinsler quickly fell behind, 0–2, and he has fouled away the last two pitches.

Carrasco's eighth pitch of the at-bat and Kinsler takes a rip and hits a fly ball to Jay Bruce in right field, who catches it for the first out. Alex Presley is the designated hitter in game one, and he takes strike one on a fastball. This is a little unusual not to see Presley either in right or left field. Carrasco's pitch and Presley drives a ball to deep left but foul to fall behind, 0–2. Carrasco's two-strike pitch is swung on and missed as the DH whiffs on a fastball that he chases out in front of the plate. Miguel Cabrera bats third; this is his tenth season with the Tigers, and over the years, he has been the face of this franchise and has never been an easy out against the Indians. Cabrera is walked on six pitches, and the Tigers get a two out base runner for Nick Castellanos.

On the first pitch offered to him, Castellanos hits a ball down the left field line that bounces fair and goes over the sidewall for a ground rule double, thankfully Cabrera has to stop at third base. Carrasco now faces Jeimer Candelario with two outs and runners covering second and third for the Tigers. Carrasco fires strike one as Candelario waves at the first pitch. On the 2–2 count, Carrasco's pitch is swung on, and a shallow fly ball on the infield is played by Lindor to retire the side. One strikeout for Carlos Carrasco as he strands the two runners, and Detroit does not score as the ground rule double saves a run for the Indians. Frankie Lindor, the shortstop, leads off for the Tribe; the Tigers have Myles Jaye on the mound tonight. This is just Jaye's second start of the year; he is 1–0 and Lindor takes ball one. Lindor does a great job of fouling off close pitches as Jaye moves ahead of the All-Star shortstop with one ball and two strikes.

On the ninth pitch of this at-bat, he swings right over the curveball that breaks down in front of home plate for out number one. Lonnie Chisenhall bats second; he is playing in left field tonight for the Tribe. The first pitch and Chisenhall hits a grounder to Cabrera, who flips the ball to the pitcher, Jaye, for the second out. Lindor and Chisenhall are retired, and with two outs, Jose Ramírez, the league leader in extra base hits, will bat. The first pitch is inside for a ball, and Ramírez backs away and the count is 1–0. Jaye's second pitch, and it hits Ramírez in his hand. The umpire says that it hit the bottom of his bat for a strike, and Francona bounds out of the dugout and has some choice words for home plate umpire Paul Emmel. But a replay review sends Ramírez to first base, and the first inning continues as Encarnacion steps up for his first at-bat. Edwin Encarnacion swings at the first pitch and lines a base hit into left field, and the Indians now have runners on first and second.

Jay Bruce, the right fielder, will take his first swings, looking to score first as the Indians have done in nearly every game during this streak. Jaye's pitch and Bruce hits a ball right to Tyler Collins in left field for the third out; that ends the first inning. The Tigers' catcher will grab a bat next as James McCann is the leadoff batter; we have no score in the top of the second inning. Carlos Carrasco launches his first pitch, and it is too low for ball one. In the series in Detroit, McCann had a hot bat while playing in two games and batting five for seven off Indians' pitchers. The 1–0 pitch and McCann hits a grounder that gets beyond the diving Lindor and rolls into left center for a leadoff single. That is the second hit for the Tigers, and now Tyler Collins will take his first swings with a man on first base. Two quick strikes on Collins as Carrasco zips the heater in for a 0–2 count. Carrasco delivers his third pitch to Collins, and McCann is running with the pitch, and it is a swing and a miss! Carrasco's changeup stays up in the zone, but he gets away with that mistake. With one out, the Tigers now have McCann camping on second base.

The center fielder, JaCoby Jones, is batting with the go-ahead run on second base after the single and a stolen base. Jones takes the first two pitches for balls, and for Carrasco, that last pitch really could have gone either way. The 2–0 pitch and Jones hits the ball to right field but foul, as Jay Bruce has no play. Carrasco's next pitch is delivered, and Jones takes another swing, this time missing, and the count moves back even at 2–2. Here comes the fifth pitch of this at-bat but first a throw to Ramírez to make sure McCann doesn't go too far. The 2–2 pitch, and it is a swing and a miss by JaCoby Jones! Carrasco gets him to chase his cutter breaking inside, and he misses over the top for his third strikeout.

Next up is Dixon Machado, the shortstop batting ninth and who has fallen behind, 0–2. As McCann runs for third, here is the pitch and another swing and a miss! Carlos Carrasco, after James McCann starts the inning with a base hit, strikes out the side, retiring all three batters on swinging strikeouts. Four strikeouts after two innings for "Cookie"; no score and the Indians are coming to bat. Carlos Santana is the leadoff man and works ahead in the count on Jaye, two balls and one strike. Myles Jay's fourth pitch is high and inside for ball three, and Santana is sitting in the box with a good hitter's count. Santana can be a little selective here, but if a pitch is right over the plate, expect him to connect. Jay's 3–1 pitch is offered, and it is low for ball four; Carlos Santana gets walked to begin the bottom of the second inning. That is the first walk by Jaye and the third base runner for Cleveland.

Yandy Díaz, batting now, takes the first pitch as it is off the plate for ball one. Five of the last six pitches have not been in the strike zone for Jaye; his second pitch is gift-wrapped to Díaz, who slaps a base hit into left field for a single. Carlos Santana stays at second, and Yan Gomes will bat with two men on and nobody out. Jaye's first offering to Gomes and he lines a broken bat base hit into center field; coming home is Santana, and it is 1–0 Tribe. Cleveland Indian's catchers stay hot as Gomes and Pérez have both played in nine games each during this streak; that is Gomes's tenth RBI with three home runs and a seven-game hit streak. Also, give Yan Gomes his fiftieth RBI this year. Díaz is on second, Gomes on first, and nobody is out for the center fielder, Greg Allen. The first pitch by Jaye and Allen squares to bunt, and he pushes it down the third base side, and everyone is safe! The bases are loaded for Francisco Lindor, and there is nowhere to put him, and what's worse for Myles Jaye is there are no outs. On the first pitch to Lindor, he is taking all the way, and Myles Jaye falls behind, 1–0.

"Here's the pitch, a swing and a line drive gapper right center gets down goes to the wall. Díaz scores, Gomes scores, look at Allen flying scoring! Lindor headfirst slide at third it's a triple! Ball gets away backed up near the stands by the pitcher Jaye," comments Tom Hamilton.

On one swing, Frankie Lindor hits a bases-clearing triple to extend the Indians' lead. The Clevelanders now are leading by four here in the second, and still there is nobody out. Lonnie Chisenhall bats a second time this game, and he is 0–1 with a groundout. The Indians have Lindor standing on third, looking to add another run, maybe two. The pitch and Chisenhall hits a ball at Dixon Machado, who looks over to third to keep Lindor at bay as he throws Chisenhall out and Lindor can't come home. Ramírez is now the batter, and he is 0–0 since he got hit by a pitch in the hand, his first time up, and was left stranded on base.

In the previous series for José Ramírez in Detroit, in the fourth game, he was hitting everything. He went 5–5 with two home runs and three doubles in a game where he had three RBIs in the 11–1 win. It is an even count now; on Ramírez, as he swings and sends a flyball to medium deep center, Jones grabs it and Lindor tags from third as the throw home is not in time, and in sliding safely on the sac fly is Lindor. For the Indians, all five men that bat reach base and come all the way home to score for a five-run second inning. Encarnacion grounds out to Dixon Machado to end the inning, but the scoring has begun here in the bottom of the second. With the scoreboard reading, 5–0, the Tribe leads the Tigers. Ian Kinsler leads off the top of this third inning for Detroit, his team trailing by five after the big second inning by the Indians. Carrasco's first pitch is swung on by Kinsler, and this ball is lined to center field for a leadoff base hit. In the top of the second inning, James McCann started the inning with a single, but Carrasco fanned the next three batters.

Alex Presley is now the batter; he is 0–1 as he struck out in the first inning. The tally is one ball and two strikes on Presley after he fouls away the second and third pitches. One of them, that tough cutter that breaks away from the hitter, it is a beautiful pitch. Carrasco offers, and Presley swings and chops the ball to Ramírez, who decides to get the sure out at first. Kinsler moves up to second with one out. Miguel Cabrera will bat for a second time today; he was walked by Carrasco and eventually made it to third but did not score. Cabrera works the count full, and he is trying to get a hit and score Kinsler from second with one out. The payoff pitch to Cabrera, it is a swing and a foul tip into the glove of Yan Gomes! Carlos Carrasco, with another strikeout, gives him five in two and two-thirds innings. Nick Castellanos faces Carrasco a second time; he doubled but was left stranded in the first inning. His ground rule double in the first inning saved a run for Cleveland. Here is his first pitch, and Castellanos pops this ball on the infield, a floater that Ramírez squeezes in the glove for the third out.

For two consecutive innings, the Tigers get a leadoff base hit but do not score. Carrasco delivers with another zero, and he has struck out five batters, all who have gone down swinging. In the bottom of the third, the Indians do not add to their five-run lead. Carlos Santana reaches base on a one out, throwing error by Ian Kinsler; Díaz and Gomes are retired on a line out and groundout. In the top of the fourth inning, Carrasco again allows a leadoff hit, but again Carrasco recovers, and the Tigers left men stranded on base. Carrasco gets his sixth strike out, and Detroit has left six base runners stranded after four innings. The starter, Myles Jaye, stays in the game. He has given up five runs, all of them earned. Greg Allen batting, he is 1–1 with an infield bunt single, and he scored in the second inning on the bases-clearing triple by Lindor. Allen swings at the first pitch, and the ball rolls away from first; Cabrera plays it and flips the ball to the pitcher Jaye for the first out.

Francisco Lindor steps to the plate with one out with the Indians leading the Tigers, 5–0, and he has three RBIs and a run scored. The first pitch is offered, and Lindor hits a hard grounder near second; the ball glances off Kinsler's glove and makes its way into right field and is ruled a hit. Lindor is now two for three with a triple and a single. Myles Jaye faces the next batter and has Chisenhall behind 1–2. He grounded out in his first plate appearance. Jaye's pitch is called strike three by the home plate umpire, and that is his second strikeout of the day. Now José Ramírez bats for the third time today; he is 0–1 with a sacrifice fly that scored the team's fifth run. Lindor is still the runner on first; he has stolen fourteen bases and has been caught three times this year. The first offering by Jaye and Ramírez swings and smokes this ball deep to right field, down the line it goes and…gone!

A two-run lined shot over the right field wall, and the major leaguer with more extra base hits than any player in the game (79) hits his twenty-sixth home run! The score is now 7–0, and the Indians are pounding the Detroit Tigers. It was mentioned before how tough of an out Ramirez was in Detroit when hitting all those home runs, and now he does it to Detroit on the Indians' home turf. The Tigers have seen enough and make a pitching change and call on Zac Reininger from the bullpen. Myles Jaye's final numbers are three and two-thirds innings pitched and allowed seven earned runs. An error and a walk prolongs the inning, but Carlos Santana flies out to Collins in left for the third out. The Tribe is in command as they add two more runs on the Ramírez blast, 7–0, after four innings in Cleveland. As we move to the top of the fifth inning, Carlos Carrasco has given up six hits, but so far, the scoreboard shows all zeros for the Tigers. He also adds another strikeout, giving him seven for the game as Miguel Cabrera strikes out for a second time.

After a scoreless fifth, Zac Reininger stays on the mound for the Tigers, and he only pitched one-third of an inning when he took over for Myles Jaye in the fourth inning. A single by Díaz and an infield hit by Gomes starts the bottom of the fifth inning with the score 7-0 Cleveland in front. Greg Allen bats now with two men on base; he singled and came home to score on the bases-clearing triple in the second inning. Allen works the count full, and on the next pitch, Greg Allen drives the ball high, and deep to the left center field gap, Jones leaps at the wall and robs Allen of at least a double and a run. Díaz tags up and advances to third on that nice catch by JaCoby Jones, and now coming in from the on-deck circle with one out is Francisco Lindor. The Tribe shortstop is having another big day at the plate; he is two for three with three runs driven in and has scored twice on a sac fly and a home run ball. As he steps in, there is one out for Lindor, with runners at the corners. Lindor takes the first pitch, and it is a ball from Zac Reininger. The 1–0 offering is delivered, and Lindor slowly chops the ball to Ian Kinsler who records the force out at second, but Díaz comes home from third to make it 8–0 Indians.

Lindor beats the return throw by Machado, which would have been a double play, so the Tigers only record one out. For the game, Lindor now has four RBIs and a season total of seventy-seven. We move to the top of the sixth inning now with Carrasco pitching a gem of a game with seven strikeouts. James McCann lines out on a ball hit sharply to Greg Allen in center after Jeimer Candelario singles to Jay Bruce to start the inning. Tyler Collins, the left fielder, steps to the plat batting, 1–2, in this game as he has singled and struck out. Carrasco fires strike one as Collins decides to take the pitch over the plate. Carrasco's next pitch is high for a ball and evens the count. Collins fouls away the third pitch on what looks like a changeup, and he is in a hole 1–2 and in danger of striking out for a second time. Carrasco sends the pitch, and Collins swings and misses on the fastball! Carrasco, with eight strikeouts in the contest now, has given Detroit all they can handle from the mound tonight. That is also Carrasco's two hundredth strikeout of this season, the second starter on the Indians' roster with two hundred or more strikeouts along with Corey Kluber.

Working quickly to the next batter, JaCoby Jones swings and misses for strike three to end the top of the sixth inning; Carrasco now has piled up nine strikeouts as he doesn't wait to climb above the two-hundred mark. The Tigers once again reach base, but another shutout inning pitched by Carlos Carrasco and the Indians are nine outs away from winning their nineteenth straight ball game. We are now in the bottom of the eighth inning, and the Indians are leading now, 9–0, when they scored on a bases-loaded groundout in the sixth that Díaz hit as the Tigers fail to get the inning ending double play. Here in the eighth, Erik González gets his second at-bat, and he is 0–1 as he batted for the first time in the bottom half of the sixth as a pinch hitter. Jairo Labourt is summoned to be the Tiger's fourth reliever of this game. Erik González takes the first pitch for a strike, and he falls behind in the count, 0–1.

Labourt's 0–1 offering is launched to González, and he hits this ball to the shortstop Dixon Machado, who bobbles it to allow González to reach first base safely on the error. Abraham Almonte gets his first action of the day, as he came in to run for Encarnacion. With this big a lead, Terry Francona can afford to make these changes and rest some of the regulars. Lindor is out of the game, and so are Gomes and Bruce; it is one of those games where everyone might get a chance to log some innings. Abraham Almonte works to a 3–1 count, so he can be selective on the next offering. Jairo Labourt delivers, and his pitch is inside for ball four; Almonte takes his base, and Erik González advances to second. Two men on for Tyler Naquin, 9–0, Indians dominating here in the late innings and are on their way to continuing this historical streak.

With nobody out, Naquin swings on the first pitch and finds a gap in right field, and both runners advance and hold; the Indians have the bases loaded for the second time in three innings. Brandon Guyer steps into the batter's box, and he replaces Chisenhall in the outfield and gets his first at-bat with the bases full and nobody out. The pitcher Labourt is in a heap of trouble with Indians on every base, and his team is already down by nine runs. The first offering to Guyer and the ball gets away from the catcher, and González comes home to make it 10–0 Indians. On the 1–0 pitch, Guyer hits a ball to the left fielder Tyler Collins, who catches it for the out as Almonte comes home on the sac fly to run the score to 11–0 here in the eighth. This is the fifth time the Indians have played the Tigers during this streak and the third time they have scored ten or more runs. In the top of the ninth inning, what will likely be the Tigers' last batter is Andrew Romine, facing Zach McAllister with two strikes.

"First at bat for Andrew Romine he'll bat lefthanded. Sends a high fly, shallow left coming hard Guyer near the line makes the catch the Indians left fielder squeezes it, ball game! The Indians relentless pursuit of a potential major league record winning streak continues onward. Nineteen in a row for the Indians. The fourth longest winning streak in major league history," Tom Hamilton says.

Fifteen years ago, the Oakland A's set an American League record playing and winning twenty games in a row. Now the Cleveland Indians have an opportunity to match that record as they hand the baseball to one of the most dominant pitchers in the game. Corey Kluber will start for the Indians in front of this crowd of over twenty-four thousand fans. The Indians' nineteen-game winning streak started on August 24 when they beat the Red Sox, and they have not looked back since. During this run, Corey Kluber has made three starts, notching a win in every game, and has only allowed five runs in twenty-three innings pitched. Kluber has extended his record to fifteen wins against four losses, and his ERA is now well below three. He is one of the top nominees in discussion to win his second American League Cy Young Award. No pitcher in Indians history has ever been awarded the CY Young twice, but for now, his focus is on winning this ball game and being a part of team history.

Ian Kinsler will lead it off; he takes a first pitch strike, and we are underway off the shores of Lake Erie. The 0–1 pitch from Kluber and Kinsler whacks this ball down the line fair to right field; he hustles toward second and slides in safely as Kinsler starts this contest with a double. So the Tigers have an early opportunity to score first against the Tribe's ace with nobody out, and Alex Presley is the second batter. Presley shows bunt, but he pulls the bat back as Kluber misses the dish for ball one. Looks like Detroit will try to sacrifice Kinsler over to third base to get an early tally. The second pitch and now Presley gets the ball on the ground; it's bunted nicely, and Yandy Díaz has just the one play as he retires Presley at first base for the first out, and Kinsler does move over to third base. So the Tigers who know how tough it is to score against Kluber use one of the oldest tricks in the book to move the runner over, and now the first baseman, Miguel Cabrera, will look to drive him across the plate. Kluber's first pitch to Cabrera is taken for a strike, and he gets ahead in the count, 0–1.

The next pitch to Cabrera and the ball breaks down low for an even 1–1 count. Cabrera is looking for the perfect pitch to swing at; with a man on third and one out, he wants to find a way to put a tally on the board. Cabrera works ahead in the count, 3–1, but he fouls away the fifth pitch to make the count full. Kluber looks Kinsler back to third, and the payoff pitch delivered for a called strike three! A fastball on the inner corner of home plate gets Miguel Cabrera looking and gives Kluber his first strikeout and two outs. Nick Castellanos bats, and Ian Kinsler is still standing on third after he led off with a double to right field. The count is 2–2 on Castellanos, who is looking for a huge clutch two out hit to take a rare first inning lead. Kluber's 2–2 pitch is swung on and missed, and the Tigers are held scoreless in the first after getting the leadoff man aboard, but Kluber fans two batters, and the Indians will look to score first. Francisco

Lindor will get the first at-bat in the bottom of this scoreless first inning, and Matthew Boyd will pitch for the Detroit Tigers. Lindor is batting with a 2–2 count now, and Boyd is about to make the eighth pitch of this at-bat.

"Here it comes, a swing and a high drive deep left field Presley's back, on the track at the wall looking up it is gone! He's done it again, Francisco Lindor! The first Cleveland Indians shortstop to ever go deep thirty times in a season," announces Tom Hamilton.

That is the nineteenth time during this amazing streak that the Indians have scored first, and what a way to begin the game when you're chasing history. Well, now the Tribe just wants to add to the lead, especially when it is so early and when they've got a All-star like Corey Kluber on the mound. Austin Jackson will bat second; he hits this ball right back to Matthew Boyd the pitcher, who grabs it and throws out Jackson in plenty of time for the first out. José Ramírez and Edwin Encarnacion both are retired; Ramírez flies out to Presley in left, and Encarnacion lines out to Jeimer Candelario at third base. The Indians are leading, 1–0, after one inning as Frankie Lindor takes Boyd deep as we move to the top of the second. Jeimer Candelario bats to start the second inning. Kluber falls quickly behind with a 2–0 count, and his last pitch is a fastball that is too high, and he needs to bring that down in the zone.

Candelario swings at the third pitch and hits this ball to Ramírez, who throws out the runner for out number one. Tyler Collins gets his first at-bat with his team down 1–0 in the top of the second, and he is facing one of the league's best pitchers. Kluber's 1–1 offering to Collins and he hits a ground ball to Ramírez, who plays the ball on a hop and fires the ball to Santana for out number two. Bryan Holaday is the Tiger's catcher in this game, and he steps in with two outs and no base runners aboard. Kluber's first pitch and it is a strike to Holaday; Kluber is looking for a three-up, three-down second inning. Strike two is called as Kluber blows it by him and gets him to swing through it. Kluber with two strikes on Bryan Holaday looking to get his third strikeout. The pitch, Holaday swings and this ball is popped high and looping foul near first; Santana makes the play, and the side is retired. The first three-up, three-down inning for Corey

Kluber keeps the score, 1–0 Indians, after one and a half innings in Cleveland.

In the next frame, the Indians get three one-out singles from Jay Bruce, Yandy Díaz, and Brandon Guyer, but Yan Gomes becomes Boyd's first strikeout victim of the game. Up next comes Lindor, the man who gave the Tribe the lead with his solo blast, and he pops out behind home plate to end the second, and the bases stay loaded. The Tigers will bat in the top of the third, trailing Cleveland by a run. Kluber marches back to the mound, and he will face the Tigers' designated hitter, Efrén Navarro, in the top of this third inning. Kluber's pitch and it is just a bit outside. Kluber probably doesn't think so, but he always does a great job showing little emotion; one pitch usually won't affect him. The 1–0 pitch and Navarro swings and hits this ball very deep but foul for an even 1–1 count. Another foul ball, this one tipped at home plate, and Navarro is now behind one ball and two strikes. Kluber looks for the sign he fires and strike three called on Efrén Navarro! Kluber with strikeout number three and next up is Andrew Romine, who will bat with one out.

It is 1–0 Indians in the top of the third inning, and Kluber has set down seven batters in a row since Kinsler's leadoff double in the first. Romine is the ninth man in the lineup tonight playing shortstop, and he swings and sends a slow grounder near first as Carlos Santana runs toward second to play it, and he flips the ball to Kluber, covering first base for the second out. The leadoff batter, Ian Kinsler, is now batting with two outs, and the bases are empty. Kinsler, who doubled to right field his first time up, was held at third base after Corey Kluber strikes out Cabrera and Castellanos. He is looking for his second hit of the game. Kluber works ahead on Kinsler, 0-2, and he swings and misses. Although Gomes drops the ball, he recovers and throws Kinsler out, running for first to complete the fourth strikeout for Kluber.

For the second straight inning, the Detroit Tigers go in order, and Kluber, as always, is looking sharp from the outset. In the home half of the inning, Austin Jackson swings at Boyd's first pitch and smokes a line drive to left field that falls in front of Alex Presley. That is the second time in three innings that the Indians get their leadoff batter on base. José Ramírez steps in now; he is hitless so far as he flied out to Presley in the first inning. Ramírez has fallen behind, 0–2, to Matthew Boyd, and he fouls away the last pitch sharply down the right field line as he is a bit out in front of that pitch. The 0–2 to Ramírez and he swings and connects; this ball is headed to right, but this one will stay fair for a single, and Jackson will stop at second base. Two leadoff singles by Jackson and Ramírez, there is nobody out for Encarnacion, who will try to pad the lead. Edwin Encarnacion fouls back the 0–1 pitch and is now down 0–2 and trying to score Austin Jackson from second with a hit.

Here comes Boyd's third pitch to Encarnacion, and it misses away to work the count to 1–2. We are still in the bottom of the third, and it is 1–0 Cleveland who is playing for their twentieth straight win that would tie an American League record. Encarnacion looks at the next pitch but strike three called for the first out. He just lets the fastball go by and doesn't take a hack at that pitch, so he is walking back to the dugout. Carlos Santana is now the batter, and he is 0–1 for the day as he began the second inning grounding out to the shortstop, Andrew Romine. Matt Boyd's first offering to Santana and he swings and misses for strike one. Santana is now behind with no balls and two strikes with Ramírez on first, and Jackson is on second and the Tribe leading by a run. The pitch and Carlos Santana chases the changeup below the knees for Boyd's third strikeout in this game, and the runners stay where they are. Jay Bruce is the next batter, and he is 1–1 after he singled but was left stranded on third in the bottom of the second after Lindor pops out to end the inning. Bruce awaits the 3–0 pitch, and Boyd fires, and it is too low for a four-pitch walk. For the second inning in a row, the Indians will bat with the bases loaded.

There are two outs and the bases full of Indians for Yandy Díaz, who singled his first time up. He wants to put the ball in play as his team is only leading by a single run. Yandy Díaz with a chance to blow this game open and with one of the game's best pitchers on the mound, if you give Kluber a little run support, you're likely to notch a win. Here comes the pitch from Matt Boyd, and Yandy swings and sends a fly ball to deep right field but not deep enough. Castellanos catches the ball in front of the track, and the Indians leave the bases loaded again. We move to the top of the fourth inning, and Kluber goes back to work with a slim 1–0 lead. The left fielder Alex Presley gets his second at-bat, he bunted Kinsler to third base after Kinsler started the first inning with a double, but Kinsler never scored. Kluber tosses the eighth pitch of this at-bat to Presley with the count at 3–2, and the last two pitches were fouled back. The payoff pitch is on its way from Kluber, and Presley hits the ball, and it bounces in front of the plate right back to Kluber, who grabs it and throws to Santana to get Presley and the first out in the inning. That is ten batters in a row that Kluber has sent back to the first base dugout; he has been cruising since he allowed the double from Ian Kinsler.

Miguel Cabrera is the batter now, and the Tigers have only one hit since they got the leadoff double to start the game. The first pitch to Miguel Cabrera is offered, and he swings and misses at the fastball; Kluber gets ahead, 0–1. There is nobody on for the Tigers, and Kluber's next pitch is made, and it is high and inside; Cabrera leans back as that pitch is inside and tight. Cabrera is in a good position now with a 3–1 count, and Kluber has not walked a batter yet in the eleven he has faced. Kluber's 3–1 offering and Cabrera swings and connects. This ball is hit just wide of the third base bag, but it is foul for a full count. Kluber sets and delivers, and it is a swing and a miss! Strike out number five for Corey Kluber, and that is the second time in this ball game Cabrera is a strikeout victim, once looking and now going down swinging. With the first two batters gone, it is up to Nick Castellanos; he is 0–1 on the day he struck out to end the first inning. Castellanos fouls back the first pitch from Kluber and gets ahead, and again the count is 0–1.

The next pitch is delivered, and Castellanos swings and smashes this ball into right field; it will go to the wall for a two-out double for Detroit's second hit. Trying to drive in a run, it is an even 2–2 count on Candelario; he is 0–1 as he grounded out to Ramírez in the second inning. Castellanos takes off from second with the pitch, but with a called strike three on Jeimer Candelario, the inning is over! After three and a half innings, Corey Kluber has struck out six batters while allowing only two hits. With the Indians leading by a run, they are slowly making their way toward history, and with this Ace on the mound, most fans wouldn't bet against them, even with this small lead.

On to the bottom of the fourth inning and two batters are down for Francisco Lindor; he has homered and popped out behind home plate. Tip your cap to Matt Boyd; during this incredible streak the Indians are on, usually when the Tribe has scored, their bats explode. But the Indians haven't done anything since the leadoff home run by Lindor, and twice they have left the bases loaded. The pitch to Lindor, he swings and hits a line drive right to the center fielder, Tyler Collins, who nabs it to retire the side in order. That is the first time Boyd and the Tigers retire the Indians in order, and the score remains 1–0 Cleveland as we head to the top of the fifth inning. Tyler Collins bats with a fresh count and a fresh inning, trying to get a spark going for him and his team as they trail by a run in the middle innings. Collins is 0–1 on the day, and he grounded out to José Ramírez in his first at-bat in this game. Kluber gets ahead of Collins, 1–2, and he has fanned six Tiger batters already. There is a "ground ball to first, diving backhanded stop by Santana makes a good feed to Kluber for out number one" (Matt Underwood).

The Tigers catcher steps in, and Kluber quickly gets ahead of Bryan Holaday with strike one. Holaday is 0–1 on the day, and Kluber in four and one-third innings throws pitch number 67, so at this rate, he can definitely pitch deep into the game. The pitch and Holaday hits the ball up the middle, and Lindor grabs it in the outfield grass, spins, throws—he gets him! Game after game these fans see this young man make the gold glove effort, and he just did it again. Also, on that play, there is a great grab on the back end by Carlos Santana. Now there are two outs for the Tigers in this fifth inning, and they have been robbed of two base hits so far as Corey Kluber and the Tribe defense are one out away from putting up another zero on the scoreboard.

Efrén Navarro swings and hits a fly ball to medium deep left field, and Guyer backs up a bit and makes the catch for the third out. The Tribe defense pays dividends for Kluber and the Indians, and they take away two hits from the Tigers while flashing some leather as Lindor makes a big play defensively. Austin Jackson grabs a bat in the bottom of the fifth inning with his team leading the Tigers, 1–0. Jackson has grounded out and singled to left, and he wants to start this inning off with a base knocker so his team can add on to the lead. Matthew Boyd blows a strike past Jackson, and he swings and seems as if he is trying to hit that ball into Lake Erie. The next pitch and Jackson hits this ball right back to Boyd on the mound who grabs it on a bounce and throws him out. One out for José Ramírez, he singled in his last plate appearance but was left stranded. The first offering from Boyd and Ramírez hits a sharp liner off the bat to the shortstop Romine, who fields the ball cleanly and gets Ramírez for out number two. The Indians DH is the next batter, and Edwin Encarnacion is down in the count, 1–2. He waves at the next pitch, and that is a strikeout for Boyd, who retires the Indians in order in the bottom of the fifth inning. That is the second straight at-bat that Edwin strikes out and give Matthew Boyd five on the day. He has been in command of the Indians hitters ever since Lindor took him deep in the bottom of the first.

Detroit's utilityman, Andrew Romine, leads off the sixth inning for the Tigers, and he is searching for a big leadoff hit as his team trails by a run; Detroit has just two hits off Kluber. First pitch from Kluber is a fastball that Romine swings over the top of. The second pitch and Romine drives this ball deep but foul; he jumps on that ball but gets out in front, and the count is now 0–2. Corey Kluber's pitch count is still below eighty pitches as he offers the two-strike toss to Andrew Romine. Romine turns away from what looks like a breaking ball, but it sails way inside for a ball and a 1–2 count. Yan Gomes gives Kluber the sign…here it comes and strike three called! Andrew Romine gets caught looking at a fastball, and that beauty gives Kluber strikeout number seven. Ian Kinsler is the batter now, and he is one of the two Tiger batters with a hit against Kluber. Both hits are doubles, and Kinsler even made it to third, but his teammates couldn't bring him home. The pitch and Kinsler swings, and this ball is hit right at Kluber, who snatches it and throws to Santana for out number two.

Alex Presley is now batting with the bases empty. He has grounded out two times today, once on a sacrifice bunt when he moved Kinsler from second to third. Corey Kluber prepares to make the eighth pitch to Alex Presley, and he still has not walked a batter, and we are in the top of the sixth inning. The Tigers are still behind, 1–0, thanks to this masterful performance from Corey Kluber and some great team defense. The payoff pitch, it is a swing and a miss! Rack up strikeout number eight and another zero on the scoreboard for Kluber. Alex Presley swings right through that ninety-four-mile-per-hour heater. The Indians will come to bat in the bottom of the sixth with a 1–0 lead and just nine outs away from joining the Oakland A's for the longest win streak in American League history! First, though, the Tigers have a pitching change to start the bottom of the sixth, and Blaine Hardy takes over for Matthew Boyd who pitches very well as he allows just the one run on six base hits. Carlos Santana bats for a third time in this game, and he is 0–2 with a swinging strikeout in the bottom of the third.

Hardy's first pitch to Santana and he rips a ball in the left center field gap; it will go all the way to the wall, and Santana slides into second safely ahead of the throw from Presley. The Indians get their first leadoff hit since the third inning and continue leading the Tigers by just a run, so they want to keep the line moving. Jay Bruce is batting, he singled to right field in the second inning and was left stranded on base, along with Díaz and Guyer. Bruce is behind Hardy, 0–2; the next offering and he hits a grounder to Cabrera at first, and Santana will move up on the out at first. Bruce doesn't drive him in, but he moves him over, and they have two outs to play with. Yandy Díaz falls behind in the count, a ball and two strikes, with Santana running at third base with one out. Blaine Hardy delivers to Díaz, who takes a swing and a miss, and he chases the curveball inside, and now there are two outs. A second pitching change is made for the Tigers, and Drew VerHagen is called on to try and keep this a 1–0 ball game here in the sixth. The Indians bring on a pinch hitter, Francisco Mejía, who will bat for Brandon Guyer, an interesting move by Tito, especially in a ball game that has not yet been decided.

Now the Tigers intentionally walk the rookie catcher, so Drew VerHagen can pitch to Yan Gomes, who has really swung the bat well lately. With runners at the corners and two out and the Tribe with a 1–0 lead, VerHagen's first pitch takes a bounce off catcher Bryan Holaday's mitt. Santana alertly races home from third, and he slides in safely! There is the insurance run the Indians have been searching for. They increase the lead, 2–0, on a wild pitch, and Santana comes home to score. One out in the top of the seventh inning and with Castellanos running at first and Jeimer Candelario batting, the Indians have a two-run lead, and Corey Kluber pitching one heck of a game. Here comes the payoff pitch, and Candelario swings, and this ball is driven to Lindor, who steps on second, throws to first, and it is an inning ending double play! Seven shutout frames from Kluber and listen to this crowed roar; they know what is at stake. Corey Kluber has made ninety-three pitches, and the Tigers are having a difficult time figuring him out. It is the top of the ninth inning at Progressive Field with the Indians leading Detroit, 2–0, with one out and Ian Kinsler batting with the bases empty.

"Ian Kinsler swings at the first pitch, a one hopper to Ramírez long throw off balance and he got him! José Ramírez, falling to the seat of his pants as his momentum carried into right field got enough on that throw to nail Kinsler by a half a step!" Matt Underwood comments.

The left fielder Alex Presley faces Kluber with two gone. He is hitless today, and the Tigers, in a two-run deficit, are down to their last out. Kluber sends his pitch, and Presley swings and hits this ball deep to center field. Greg Allen races to the wall, and the ball hits the wall, and Presley is into second without a throw. Miguel Cabrera will bat next with the runner; in scoring position, he is the tying run at home plate with his team down by two. So far today he has no hits in three at-bats. The first pitch to Cabrera is swung on and missed for strike one, just two more strikes to go to put this game to bed.

"Here's the 1–1 pitch to Cabrera, a swing and a bouncer to third Urshela gloves, throws, ball game! A record tying night in Cleveland! The Indians have matched the American League record! They have won twenty in a row! The second team in the history of the American League to win twenty straight! Joining the Oakland A's of 2002 and could it end any more appropriately with Corey Kluber besting Miguel Cabrera representing the tying run at the plate?!" Tom Hamilton declares.

The fans are up on their feet at the Corner of Carnegie and Ontario—all 29,346 of them. It is a noon game in Downtown Cleveland, and the Tribe faithful are hoping to witness their ball club win a game that will put their team in the record books. Yesterday, on September 12, the Cleveland Indians won their twentieth consecutive game that tied the American League record for the longest winning streak. Corey Kluber got the win last night as he pitched a complete game shutout, striking out eight batters and retiring Miguel Cabrera, who represented the tying run at the plate in the ninth. This is the final game of the series between the Indians and the Tigers, and they won't be meeting in the playoffs. Mike Clevinger will start for the Tribe, and Ian Kinsler will bat first. The first pitch by Clevinger is taken for a strike, and we are underway off the shores of Lake Erie. Mike Clevinger is pitching today with a record of 9–5 and an ERA below 3.50. The next pitch is also taken, and this time it is low, and the count is even 1–1. This will be the fifth pitch to Kinsler, as he fouled back two straight and is behind, 1–2. Clevinger sets, delivers a swing and a miss! With the first man he faces today, Clevinger gets his first strike out on a fastball that is up in the zone, and he swings under it.

Alex Presley is now batting, and playing in left field, he got one hit in game two against Corey Kluber. Mike Clevinger's first pitch and Presley swings and punches a single to left field for the Tigers' first hit, allowing the next batter, Miguel Cabrera, to bat with a man on first and one out. The count is even, 2–2, on Cabrera, and Presley is the runner at first but doesn't attempt to steal second. The pitch, a swing and a lazy pop-up drifting near the first base seats, and José Ramírez calls off Bruce and Santana and makes the catch. Two base runners are on now for Jeimer Candelario as Clevinger walks Nick Castellanos on seven pitches. Clevinger sends his first pitch, and he gets Candelario to swing through it for a 0–1 count. Roberto Pérez calls for the pitch, and the breaking ball falls in low to even the count at 1–1. With a 2–2 count, now Clevinger's pitch to Candelario is delivered, and the batsman swings and hits this ball in the gap. It will fall for a two-out RBI double.

Alex Presley scores from second, Castellanos will hold at third base, and the Tigers go up, 1–0. James McCann is the sixth man to bat in the inning, and Clevinger has made over twenty pitches, but he has McCann down, 0–2. Here comes his pitch, and it is a swing and a miss! The Tigers do take a 1–0 lead on the double by Candelario, but Clevinger gets two strikeouts and keeps two base runners stranded in scoring position. The Indians will take their first attempts in the bottom of the first trailing, 1–0. Francisco Lindor leads off against Detroit's starting pitcher, Buck Farmer, who is 4–2 on the season with a high ERA above six. The Indians are trailing by a run, just the second time in the last twenty games that they haven't scored first. Twelve days ago, when the Indians hitters faced Farmer, he allowed five runs in three innings, and the Indians beat the Tigers, 10–0. Today Farmer makes his first pitch, and Lindor hits a hard grounder into right field into the corner for a leadoff double, and the tying run is on base. Lonnie Chisenhall is second in the lineup today, and he falls behind, 0–1, as he swings and misses at Farmer's first pitch. Chisenhall is now behind, 0–2, as he takes a pitch that he thinks is low, but it gets called a strike.

The next pitch to Chisenhall is offered, and he swings and hits it down the line but foul, and the count remains 0-2. Lindor is still the runner at second base, the pitch, and Lonnie swings and misses for strike three and the first out. Now Buck Farmer is facing José Ramírez, who leads the majors in extra base hits. Ramírez takes a low fastball for ball one as he gets ahead of Farmer. The 1–0 to Ramírez comes in, and he swings and yanks this ball hard but fouls it to deep right down the line, and it is an even count. Farmer misses on the last two pitches, and Ramírez can choose to swing or take here as he is in a good hitter's count. The 3–1 is delivered for ball four, and Buck Farmer walks Ramírez, and the Indians have two men on with Encarnacion coming to bat. Edwin falls behind, 0–2, and he is swing-ing away but has not made contact on the first two pitches. Farmer delivers, and Encarnacion swings and misses for Farmer's second strikeout of the inning. The Indians trail Detroit, 1–0, in the bottom of the first, and Jay Bruce will step up and take his first at-bat.

One ball one strike on Jay Bruce, he is batting with Lindor on second and Ramírez standing on first. Farmer's twenty-fifth pitch of the inning, "a swing and a high drive this is hit to deep left center field it is gone! Hit right near the yellow line in deep left center and dropped back on the playing field, it is ruled a three-run home run! Jay Bruce with a towering blast to left center that looked like it hit right near the yellow line and bounced back into play. The Indians Jay Bruce has put the Tribe on top of this one by a score of 3–1" (Tom Hamilton). Jay Bruce, traded from the New York Mets to the Indians, was acquired in early August when the Tribe was in Tampa Bay. He has just hit a three-run home run to give the Indians a 3–1 lead in the bottom of the first. Carlos Santana strikes out to end the inning, and Farmer gets all outs via strikeouts. But the Indians bats do their job, and they take the lead after falling behind, 1–0. Jay Bruce blasts a three-run home run that just barely clears the wall in left center field. The Tigers' Andrew Romine leads off to begin the top of the second inning. Tigers are now behind the Indians 3–1.

During this incredible run in the few times the Indians have been behind on the scoreboard, they have come right back to take the lead. When you give back the lead to this team with the way they are playing right now, you're asking for trouble. Clevinger gets a strike past Romine on a check swing, but it is 0–1. Clevinger now gets ahead, 0–2, and Romine swings and hits a ball foul behind the plate. Pérez calls for the pitch, and it is a swing and a miss, but the ball is dropped, Roberto Perez plays it and throws out Romine to complete Clevinger's third strikeout. JaCoby Jones is the eighth batter in Brad Ausmus' lineup, and he will take his first swings on the day with the Tigers trailing the Indians by two. Jones swings and misses, and once again Mike Clevinger gets ahead in the count. Clevinger has become a very reliable pitcher in the Indians' rotation since late August, and he typically is able to pitch about six innings to give the Tribe some quality starts. JaCoby Jones works the count full, the payoff pitch, and strike three is called! Clevinger gets Jones looking at a changeup, and he probably expected a fastball, and now

Clevinger has four punch-outs. The third out is made on a ground ball hit by Iglesias that is played by Ramírez.

The Indians will bat again in the bottom of the second, still leading Detroit, 3–1. Buck Farmer will pitch to the Indians' third baseman, Yandy Diaz, to start the home half of the inning. The first pitch and Díaz hits a slow grounder that Andrew Romine plays well and runs to the bag himself for the first out. Tyler Naquin bats next with one out; this is his first at-bat, and the bases are empty with one man out. Buck Farmer has Naquin down in the count, and with two strikes he has chased both pitches to fall in this hole. The 0–2 from Farmer, strike three called on Tyler Naquin. Farmer now has his fourth strikeout, and he and Clevinger both have notched four punch-outs, and the Indians now have two outs in the inning. Roberto Pérez is the ninth man in the lineup and steps in with the bases empty, and Farmer works to a 0–2 count on Pérez. Roberto hit the second pitch hard but foul, and he steps back in the box, looking to continue this second inning. The pitch by Farmer and a swing and a miss by Perez and Buck Farmer puts a zero up after giving up three in the first inning. Mike Clevinger heads back to the hill for the top of the third with the Indians holding on to a 3–1 lead.

Ian Kinsler takes his second at bat, and he is 0–1 with a swinging strikeout. Clevinger makes his first pitch, and Kinsler swings and lines the ball to second, but Ramírez gets the glove up for the out. One out for Presley, he is 1–1 with a single on which he came around to score on the double to left by Jeimer Candelario. The count is even at 2–2, here comes the pitch, and Presley hits his second single into left field as it falls in front of Chisenhall for the Tigers' third hit. Miguel Cabrera bats after the one out single by Presley, and he represents the tying run in this third inning. Cabrera started this game with a pop-out near first base on which Ramírez makes an over-the-shoulder catch before the Tigers took a lead. Clevinger makes his first offering and its inside for ball one as he falls behind Cabrera. The 1–0 offering and it is Cabrera with a drive deep to right; if it is fair, it is gone…but it is foul and a long strike to even the count. Clevinger's 1–1 to Cabrera is high, but he gets the call, and Brad Ausmus is shouting from the dugout; he believes the count should be reversed and it should be 2–1 for his batter, as the manager is given a warning from the umpires.

One ball and two strikes on Miguel Cabrera, and here's the pitch, strike three is called, and he can't believe it. Cabrera believes two pitches should have gone his way, but instead Clevinger has his fifth strikeout; that's the first time he's been able to strike out Cabrera. Tigers' right fielder, Castellanos, steps to the plate again; he was walked in his first at-bat and left stranded at third base. The pitch is delivered, and he swings and smokes a grounder into center field. Alex Presley moves up to second, and Jeimer Candelario will bat with two out and two on. It is still the top of the third inning, and Clevinger is putting in a bit more work now as he just allowed the tying run to reach base. Candelario represents the go-ahead run with the Indians ahead with a 3–1 lead. A full count now on Candelario, Mike Clevinger has already walked one batter, and another one here would load the bases for the Tigers. Here comes his payoff pitch, strike three called, and he gets him staring at a slider that is down the middle for strikeout number 6!

In the bottom of the third inning, it is the top of the order for the Tribe, and Francisco Lindor is batting. He doubled in his last at-bat and scored on the Jay Bruce home run. That home run was reviewed, but there was not enough evidence to overturn the call, so that is where the score still stands, 3–1. Buck Farmer's pitch to Lindor and he hits a grounder to Kinsler for the first out to start this inning. José Ramirez is batting for a second time now, and there are two outs after Lonnie Chisenhall struck out for a second time. Ramírez will bat with the bases empty and a 3–1 Indians lead in the bottom of the third inning, a rather tight ball game that is still early in the contest. Farmer's first pitch to Ramírez is way inside and almost hits him, and the count is 1–0. In his first at-bat, Ramirez walked, and he also scored on the home run in the first inning. The second pitch and José Ramírez hits this ball deep to center field, and it will go to the wall for a two-out double. Edwin Encarnacion is 0–1 so far and steps to the plate; he is one of six strikeout victims against Buck Farmer on the day. One ball no strikes on Encarnacion batting with two outs trying to pad this 3–1 lead.

The pitch, Edwin's swing, and he skies this ball to shallow right field…it is going to fall in front of Castellanos. Ramírez will score on the RBI single, and it is 4–1 Indians in the third inning. Jay Bruce will take his second series of swings in today's game; he is 1–1 with that three-run home run. The count is full on Bruce, and the payoff pitch is delivered wide for ball four. Brad Ausmus is screaming at the home plate umpire in disbelief at the call, and he has just been ejected. In the top half of the inning, Ausmus was disagreeing with the strike zone; he believes Quinn Wolcott isn't wearing his contacts. Ausmus wants to get his money's worth for the ejection, and he won't walk away. He is giving the home plate umpire everything he has to say about why he believes his strike zone is favoring the opposition. Both Ausmus and the catcher McCann are sent to the showers, and Jay Bruce will be the base runner at first, and we are back underway. The side is retired as Yandy Díaz lines out to Presley in left field. The Indians add a run on the two-out single by Encarnacion, and the score is 4–1 Tribe.

Clevinger will go back out for the top of the fourth inning. John Hicks will take his first swings; he just took over the catching duties for Detroit after James McCann was ejected. Clevinger has six strikeouts, and he gets ahead, 0–1, as Hicks is not swinging on a pitch right over the plate. The next pitch is swung on and fouled past third base, and the count is now 0–2. John Hicks asks for time, and he steps away, and as he steps back in, Clevinger is ahead—no balls, two strikes. The 0–2 pitch and Hicks swings and hits a ball to second; Ramírez grabs it, throws, and he gets him! One out now for Andrew Romine. The first baseman is hitless on the day, and in his first at-bat, he struck out to begin the top of the second. He swings at the first pitch and pops a ball high on the infield. Ramírez will take this one for the second out, and on four pitches, Mike Clevinger has set down two batters. JaCoby Jones now bats with the bases empty; Detroit only has four hits, and they trail 4–1. Jones was called out on strikes in his first time up, and he takes ball one off the plate.

Clevinger gets the sign from his catcher; the 1–0 pitch is swung and hit to Lindor at short who fires over to Carlos Santana to retire the Tigers in order. For the second time in this ball game, the Tigers go in order as Clevinger is pitching well and holding on to this three-run advantage. It is now the top of the sixth inning in the final game between the Tigers and the Indians as they finish up this three-game series. With a 4–1 tally on the scoreboard, the Indians are leading and playing for their sixth straight sweep. A victory would set a new American League record for consecutive wins since the Athletics won twenty in a row in 2002. Miguel Cabrera leads off for the Tigers with his team still trailing; he is 0–2 on the day with a strikeout. Mike Clevinger's first pitch is a strike that the batter doesn't offer on, and Cabrera falls behind 0–1. Clevinger has two strikes on Cabrera, and he is searching for his seventh punch-out. The pitch is tendered, and Cabrera hits a grounder to Díaz, but the throw from third to first is offline, and Cabrera will get an extra free base on the throwing error by Yandy Díaz.

Nick Castellanos now bats with Cabrera standing on second base after the error on the ground ball. Clevinger's first pitch is too high for ball one, and with the Tigers down by three, the batter can be swinging away here. The 1–0 offering is made, and Castellanos smokes the ball to the gap in left center where it is played off the wall by Chisenhall. Miguel Cabrera comes home, and now Castellanos is trying for second and he beats Chisenhall's throw. The score is now 4–2 Indians, and the error comes back to hurt the Indians, and the Tigers still have no outs. After back-to-back ground ball outs by Candelario and John Hicks, Castellanos moves to third base, the Tigers still have a chance to add a second run. With a full count, Andrew Romine is seeking to drive home another run, but he will need a two-out hit. Clevinger is nearing one hundred pitches, he has thrown ninety-seven to this point. Here comes the payoff pitch and Romine shoots an RBI base hit to right field where it falls in safely. The score is now 4–3 Cleveland, and the two runs by the Tigers in the sixth get Mike Clevinger sent to the showers.

JaCoby Jones, the center fielder, will face Tribe relief pitcher, Nick Goody, who will try to keep this a one-run lead for the Indians. Jones is 0–2 with a groundout and a strike out in today's contest. Goody has Jones down 0–2, the pitch and a swing and a miss! The bullpen comes in and slams the door as the Tigers leave the tying run on first base. Three pitches made by Goody and JaCoby Jones swings and misses at all three, but in the inning, the Tigers bring this game two runs closer. The inning starts with a throwing error and an RBI double, and a single scores Castellanos. The Tigers' pitching staff keep this game close as the Indians are retired in order in the bottom of the sixth inning. Daniel Norris strikes out Carlos Santana, and Yandy Díaz and Jay Bruce lined out to Presley in left field. In the top of the seventh inning at Progressive Field, Cleveland is leading Detroit, 4–3, and Nick Goody will stay on to pitch. Yandy Díaz is being replaced by Giovanny Urshela at third base, and the Indians are nine outs away from making history. José Iglesias steps in for his third at-bat of the day, and he is officially 0–1 with a walk in the top of the fifth inning.

Goody's pitch is taken inside for ball one, and he falls behind in the count. Goody's 1–0 offering is made, and Iglesias pops this ball up near third. Urshela grabs it, and Iglesias is retired for the first out in this inning. Gio Urshela just replaced Yandy Díaz, and he makes a play on the second pitch of the inning. Ian Kinsler will face Nick Goody for the first time in this ball game; he is 0–3 after his last at-bat where he grounded into a double play in the top of the fifth. The bases are empty for the Tigers, and they remain behind 4–3 with one out. Goody fires strike one past Kinsler, who swings and misses on a heater. No balls, two strikes now as the last pitch to Ian Kinsler is lined foul into the third base seats. Goody delivers, and it is a swing and a miss by Kinsler! Goody gets his second strikeout, and after facing three batters, Tyler Olson replaces Nick Goody, who retires all three batters that he faces. Olson is the Indians' second relief pitcher, and with two outs, he will face Alex Presley, who has hit two singles so far today. The first pitch is delivered by Tyler Olson, and Presley swings and the ball is skied foul behind the plate. Pérez has a play, and he catches it to end the inning.

It is stretch time at the Corner of Carnegie and Ontario, and the Indians are leading the Detroit Tigers, 4–3. Daniel Norris will continue to pitch for the Detroit Tigers, and he has pitched two innings and retired six straight hitters with two strikeouts. Brandon

Guyer will pinch-hit for Naquin, who goes 0–2 in this game. The Indians lead by a single run and are looking to expand on the lead if they can. Norris's first pitch to Guyer and he swings immediately and hits a grounder to Kinsler, who throws him out to begin the bottom of the seventh. The catcher Roberto Pérez bats with one out and the bases empty, and he has struck out twice already. Norris jumps ahead of Pérez to make the count nothing and two, and Perez is in danger of striking out all three times today.

"The pitch, swung on hit high, hit deep to center. This ball's got a chance, gone! Roberto Pérez clears the nineteen-foot wall in dead center! He has hit his fifth home run in the last fourteen games!" Tom Hamilton declares.

That is the second home run hit in this game by the Indians, and four of their five runs have come from the long ball. Jay Bruce homered in the first inning when the Indians were down, 1–0, but since then, like most of the games in the streak, they just pull away. As we move to the top of the ninth inning in Cleveland, it is still a 5–3 Tribe lead in the final game of this series against the Tigers. Cody Allen strikes out Tyler Collins, who is called to pinch-hit for JaCoby Jones. José Iglesias steps to the plate and on two pitches gets down in the count 0–2; he is hitless so far on the day. Cody Allen's pitch is swung on and hit to left field, and Chisenhall will grab it, and there are two down in the ninth.

"One out away from making history are the 2017 Cleveland Indians. It's 5–3 Tribe, Allen into the motion the wind and the pitch. Swung on ripped to left Chisenhall coming on slides, he made the catch, ball game! And mark it down folks, history on September 13 of 2017! The Cleveland Indians have set a new American League record winning their twenty-first consecutive ball game! The Indians stop the Tigers, 5–3! A winning streak that began for the Indians on August 24, still has no end to it! Twenty-one in a row by the Tribe, a new American League record matching the Chicago Cubs' twenty-one-game winning streak of 1935," Tom Hamilton remarks.

Chapter 7

The Walk-off!

From Progressive Field in Downtown Cleveland, Ohio, it is game number 147. As the Indians take the field for the pregame warm-ups, the near sellout crowd is up on their feet and roaring as the Indians prepare to begin this three-game series against the Kansas City Royals. Listening to this crowd here in Cleveland, you might think we are ready to play some October baseball. But this anxious mass is hoping to witness an Indian's victory that would break the record for the longest win streak in Major League Baseball with no ties. In yesterday's 5–3 win against the Tigers, the Indians became just the second team in Major League Baseball to win twenty-one straight games since the Chicago Cubs did it back in 1935. Josh Tomlin takes the mound for Cleveland, and Whit Merrifield leads off for the Royals and takes ball one and we are underway at the corner of Carnegie and Ontario.

The Indians last faced the Royals in a division series from August 25 through the 27 where the Clevelanders shut out Kansas City in all three games by a combined score of 20–0. It is now September 14, and they have not lost a game since that August 23 game against the Red Sox. The 1–0 pitch is delivered to Merrifield, and he swings and pops a ball high on the infield where José Ramírez will grab it for the first out of the game. Now Lorenzo Cain will grab a bat to try to get his team going early in the contest. On Tomlin's first pitch to Cain, he fires a strike at the knees, and it is a 0–1 count. The 0–1 pitch is swung on and fouled into the stands for a 0–2 count as Cain hits that slider far and hard; but too early and the ball can't find fair territory.

Tomlin's next pitch and Cain hits this ball to center field, not deep, and Abraham Almonte catches it for out number two. Melky Cabrera is the third man to bat in this first inning, and Tomlin has retired the first two batters he has faced. Cabrera gets down early in the count, 0–2, swinging and fouling off both pitches. The 0–2 pitch and Cabrera takes a ball that is too low to make the count, 1–2. Tomlin's fourth pitch to Cabrera and strike three is called on a fastball that just tickles the outer half of the plate. It is a strong first inning by Josh Tomlin; no Royals reach base, and now the Indians will take their first swings of the game. It is the bottom of the first inning, no score, and Royal starting pitcher Jakob Junis faces the shortstop Francisco Lindor to start the bottom of the first inning. Lindor takes a first pitch strike to fall behind in the count. The 0–1 pitch to Lindor, he swings and grounds a ball to Eric Hosmer at first, who fields it and flips the ball to the pitcher, Junis, covering the base for the first out. Lonnie Chisenhall steps in, batting with one out, and the bases are empty. With the first pitch, Lonnie swings, and another ball grounds on the infield, this one to second base.

The Royals' number 15, Merrifield, grabs it and makes the throw to Hosmer in time for the second out. José Ramírez bats with the bases empty, and he swings at the first pitch and misses to fall behind 0–1. Junis's next offering and Ramírez hits a ball to center field where it falls for the first hit of this game. Edwin Encarnacion bats with two gone and a man on, and Edwin really has been swinging a hot bat lately. The first offering to Encarnacion, and he hits another grounder to the shortstop, Alcides Escobar, who takes the sure out at first base to retire the Tribe. Both the Royals and the Indians have a quiet first inning, and now batters 4, 5, and 6 in the lineup for Kansas City will bat next. Eric Hosmer is the leadoff batter in the top of this scoreless second inning. Three balls and a strike on Hosmer, Tomlin has missed the strike zone on his last three pitches. Here comes the fifth pitch of the at-bat, ball four, and Josh Tomlin has surrendered his first base on balls.

The catcher, Salvador Perez, takes his first swings with a runner on base. Tomlin's first pitch to Perez and he lines a single into right center field for the Royals' first hit; they now have runners on first and third with nobody out. Perez is on first, and Hosmer is the runner at third, and the third baseman, Mike Moustakas, steps to the plate with a scoring opportunity early in this game. The first pitch to Moustakas is offered, and he swings right away and clobbers a grounder to Ramírez, who gets the force at second. Lindor's return throw sets down Moustakas for a four-six-three double play. The Indians get two outs, but Eric Hosmer scores from third base for a 1–0 Kansas City lead. That is the first run the Indians have allowed by the Royals in twenty-nine innings.

Brandon Moss is the next batter; the bases are now empty, but the Royals have the lead. Here is the 2–2 pitch, and Moss lines this ball to left field. Chisenhall is racing in, and he dives and makes the catch to end the inning! Tomlin walks off the mound; he has given up a run, and the Indians will play from behind in the bottom of the second inning. Jay Bruce is the leadoff batter; his team trails the Royals for the first time in this incredible winning streak. Jay Bruce swings at the first pitch, and he hits a ball on the ground directly to the first baseman, Hosmer, who scoops it up and steps on the base for the out. Five Cleveland hitters have batted, and four of them have hit into groundouts. Carlos Santana bats second in the second inning with the bases empty. Junis fires his first pitch in for a strike, and it is a 0–1 count. The next pitch and Santana hits a sharp grounder through the infield, and it gets by the infielders for the Indians' second hit.

The seventh man in the lineup today is the third baseman, Yandy Diaz. With one out and not much speed on first base, the Indians will need to put some hits together to re-tie this ball game. Díaz takes ball one from Junis, and with one out, the pitch is delivered, and Diaz swings and hits a grounder to Whit Merrifield, who forces Santana running to second, and Diaz is thrown out before he reaches first base to end the inning. The Royals keep the Indians off the board, and it remains 1–0 Kansas City as we move to the top of the third inning here in Cleveland. Alcides Escobar is the eighth man to bat in Ned Yost's lineup, and the Royals are leading the Indians by a run to begin the top of the third. Tomlin has been pitching well so far despite allowing a run. The first pitch comes in from Tomlin, and Escobar takes a called strike to fall back, 0–1, to begin the inning. The next pitch and Escobar hits a ball on the ground beyond Lindor for a leadoff single. That is the second hit of the game for the Royals, and now Alex Gordon will take his first swings of the day with a runner on first base. Gordon quickly falls behind in the count 0–2, and Josh Tomlin is looking to get his second strikeout of the game. The 0–2 pitch and Gordon swings and lines a ball in the air to left field. Chisenhall will make the grab for the first out, and the runner stays at first.

The Royals' lineup flips back to the leadoff man, Whit Merrifield; he is 0–1 in the game with an infield pop-out. There is one out, and the Royals have a runner on first base, and they are looking to drive him home and go up by two scores. The first offering by Tomlin and the pitch is inside to make the count 1–0 on Merrifield. Whit Merrifield is a very aggressive swinger, especially when he has the count in his favor early. Tomlin's second pitch, he swings but hits this ball to Ramírez, who grabs it and quickly throws to Lindor to force Escobar at second. Francisco Lindor makes the turn for the inning ending double play! Josh Tomlin has not had a strike out since the first inning, but he has stopped the Royals from adding on any more runs. The Indians will come to bat in the bottom of the third behind in this game, 1–0. Abraham Almonte will lead off for the Indians; he is getting his first swings in this ball game against Jakob Junis. Almonte swings at the first pitch, and he smacks this ball fair to right field and into the corner! Almonte is going for a double, the throw by Melky Cabrera is not in time, and the Indians get their first leadoff hit in the game. One out now as Yan Gomes got called out on strike three for Junis's first strikeout and out number one.

Francisco Lindor will get his second at-bat; he is 0–1 with a groundout to Eric Hosmer. Jakob Junis is ahead, 0–1, the next pitch and Lindor hits this ball deep to right field, but it hooks foul for a 0–2 hole. Two strikes on Lindor, the next pitch and he swings, and this ball is hit to center field but right at Cain, who plays it perfectly, and the Indians now have two outs. Lonnie Chisenhall is the batter, and Abe Almonte is the runner on second base after the leadoff double to right field, but now there are two outs in the inning. Chisenhall is batting with a 1–0 count; he is trying to get a clutch two out hit that will tie this ball game here in the third.

"The 1–0, swung on line drive base hit to right. Almonte will try to score, Cabrera charges, gloves, throw to the plate way up the third base line, scoring Almonte. Perez throw to second slide, tag out at second is Chisenhall," Tom Hamilton comments.

So the inning is over, and Chisenhall is out at second, but Abe Almonte comes home to tie the game at one run a piece as we move to the top of the sixth inning in Cleveland. Whit Merrifield will bat for a third time in this game; he is 0–2 with a pop-out and a ground-out. Tomlin is working ahead, 0–2, as he makes his next pitch, and Merrifield hits a fair ball down the right field line all the way to the corner. Merrifield sprints to second base, and he will get a leadoff stand-up double. The center fielder, Lorenzo Cain, steps in with the go-ahead run standing on second base with no outs. Josh Tomlin makes the first pitch. "He squibs it right out in front of the plate. Gomes looks to third throws there and they got him, what a play by Yan Gomes! Heads up, alert, and a perfect strike to Díaz at third base!" Matt Underwood exclaims. So it is a risk when you don't go for the sure out, but Yan Gomes is quick and makes a quality throw to his third baseman to get the lead runner. Melky Cabrera bats for a third time, and he is 0–2 against Josh Tomlin today. It is an even count, and on the third pitch to Cabrera, he hits a ball sharply on the ground to first base, and Santana snatches it and throws a beebee to get the lead runner, Cain, at second for a second force-out; they don't get the double play.

With two outs for the Royals in the top of the sixth, Melky Cabrera is running at first base. Two straight force-outs keep the Royals from having a big inning, and we are still tied at one with two outs, and the go-ahead runner is at first. The first baseman, Eric Hosmer, is the batter, and he looks to continue the top half of this sixth inning. Tomlin falls behind 2–0, and on the next pitch, Hosmer swings and hits a ball high and down the left field line…Almonte slides, but the ball falls in for a hit. Hosmer gets the go-ahead two out RBI, and the Royals retake the lead, 2–1. That is just the second time during this streak the Indians have lost the lead in the fifth inning or later. Back on August 28, the Yankees took a 2–1 lead over the Indians in the bottom of the fifth inning, but the Tribe came out on top, 6–2. As we move to the bottom of the eighth inning, the Royals pitcher, Mike Minor, who replaced the starter Jakob Junis in the sixth, will be replaces by reliever Ryan Buchter. The Indians still trail by a run late in this ball game, and the Royal's bullpen is just six outs away from ending this twenty-one-game win streak.

Starting off this inning for the Tribe is Frankie Lindor, and he is hitless in all three of his at-bats in this game. Buchter's first pitch and Lindor aggressively swings and lines a ball to center field, but Lorenzo Cain snares it for the first out. Francisco Lindor is having a very quiet game as he is now 0–4. Down to their final five outs, Greg Allen will make his second plate appearance. He replaced Lonnie Chisenhall in the fifth inning, who left the game with a leg injury. Allen is batting with a full count, and he hasn't yet had a good pitch to take a swing at. The payoff pitch is way up and out of the strike zone, and the Indians get the tying run on board with the speedy Greg Allen walking to first base. José Ramírez, the league leader in doubles, will take his swings next, and he now represents the go-ahead run at the plate. The pitch, Ramírez swings and sends this ball on a line to left field where it falls beyond Gordan's reach for a double. Allen will be stopped by third base coach Mike Sarbaugh, and the Indians have a great scoring opportunity.

The Royals make the decision to intentionally walk Edwin Encarnacion to load the bases for the right fielder Jay Bruce. The Tribe needs to score at least a run in the next five outs to extend their streak, and with the bases loaded and one out, the entire crowd is on their feet. Ryan Buchter makes his first pitch to Bruce, and Cleveland's right fielder swings and pops up a foul ball behind home plate that Royals' catcher Salvador Perez grabs for the second out. The bases are still loaded with Indians as Carlos Santana steps up to bat with his team trailing 2–1 in the eighth. It is an even 1–1 count on Santana; Buchter's pitch and this ball is hit and popped up. The first baseman Hosmer has room near the Royals' dugout and will grab it for the third out. The Indians load the bases with less than two outs down a run but cannot find a way to get the big hit. The Royals retain the slim one-run lead as we go to the top of the ninth inning at Progressive Field.

Tyler Olson stays in the game to pitch for Cleveland; he came in for Nick Goody after there were two outs in the top half of the eighth inning. The Indians are going to need to put up a zero in the ninth to have the best chance possible of tying or winning this game in the bottom half of the inning. Tyler Olson does his job, three up, three down go the Royals, and the score stays at 2–1 as we move to the bottom half of the last inning and the Tribe's improbable twenty-one-game winning streak is on the line. Kelvin Herrera is the new pitcher for Kansas City, and he wants to slam the door on these Cleveland Indians. Yandy Díaz remains without a hit today, and he starts the inning with a leadoff groundout to the shortstop Escobar, who throws to his first baseman in time for the first out. Tyler Naquin is called by Tito to step in as a pinch hitter with one out in the ninth, and Francona will have him hit for Brandon Guyer. Herrera is ahead of Naquin with one ball and two strikes, and the Tribe is down to their last four strikes to extend their streak. Herrera makes his fourth pitch to the Indians outfielder, and Naquin gets a piece of the ball to stay alive with a 1–2 count. Perez, the catcher, signals the next pitch, and Tyler Naquin slaps a one-out single into left for a hit! Tyler Naquin is now the game tying run at first base, and Francisco Mejía will bat for the first time, replacing Yan Gomes, as Francona continues to pull strings.

The Royals are in front in the bottom of the ninth here in Cleveland, trying to snap a twenty-one-game win streak from their division rivals. The 1–1 pitch, Mejíah swings and grounds this ball to second baseman Whit Merrifield, who tosses the ball to Escobar for one out but can't make the turn in time for the double play to end the game. The Tribe's Francisco Lindor will grab a bat as the last hope for the Indians to extend the streak. A third substitution is made by the Indians' manager, Erik González, who comes in to be the runner at first base, replacing Mejíah. Lindor battles with the Royals' pitcher, Herrera, on the first four pitches, and the Tribe is down to its last strike one more time. The next pitch is delivered, and "the 2-2, swung on drilled deep left field, Gordan back at the wall leaps...it's off the wall kicks back to left center! González scores the tying run! Lindor big turn, he'll stay at second. How about that! Frankie Lindor down to his last strike rips an RBI double the opposite way off the nineteen-foot wall in left!" (Tom Hamilton).

As clutch as a hit as you will ever see! Francisco Lindor comes through with the two-out, two-strike game, tying RBI double in the bottom of the ninth, and the fans at Progressive Field are going wild! Lindor stays stranded at second base, and the Royals end the ninth inning on a groundout hit by Austin Jackson, and for the first time in three weeks, the Indians will play some extra inning baseball. For the top of the tenth inning, the Indians call on closer Cody Allen to pitch to the Royals' hitters, and he will do what he can to keep this game tied so the Indians don't have to play from behind again. Brandon Moss is the leadoff batter, and he struck out looking in the top of the seventh inning. Cody Allen works ahead to a 0–2 count, and he blew the curveball right past him, and Moss is in a hole. The pitch by Allen, a swing and a high deep drive to right center, Tyler Naquin backpedals, and he makes the catch right against the bullpen wall without an inch of room to spare. That ball looked like it would carry further, and maybe even leave the yard, but Naquin makes the catch. The Royals have one out, and Alcides Escobar will be the hitter. The Royals gets the go-ahead run on base with a single by Escobar, but a strikeout and a groundout get Cody Allen and the Indians defense out of trouble.

We go to the bottom of the tenth in Downtown Cleveland where it is the Royals and the Indians tied at two runs apiece, and José Ramírez will lead off the inning. Brandon Maurer is the new pitcher for Kansas City, and his teammates cannot retake the lead, so he will look to match Cody Allen's doughnut on the scoreboard. The crowd continues to stand and cheer, and it is an even 1–1 count on Ramírez. Here is the pitch, and Ramírez lines a single into center, and he is trying to make it to second base. Lorenzo Cain plays the ball cleanly and throws to second, but Ramírez is safe! What hustle, that takes true guts to try for second base and test one of the better outfield arms in the game! Edwin Encarnacion bats with the winning run in scoring position and nobody out. The pitcher Maurer seems to be working around Edwin Encarnacion, and he walks him on five pitches, and Jay Bruce will bat just one swing away from driving home the winning run.

"Still nobody out in a two, two game in the tenth, Bruce awaiting the 2–0 pitch. Here it comes, a swing and a drive to deep right down the line base hit! The ball rolls into the corner, around third coming home Ramírez and it's a game winner for Jay Bruce and history marches on! A mob scene in shallow center, Jay Bruce getting pummeled! As he smoked one down the right field line a game winning single for Jay Bruce! The Indians continue this improbable run. Twenty-two consecutive wins and the Indians get their first walk off win in the streak!" Tom Hamilton exclaims.

This 3–2 win over the Royals becomes the first time in baseball history a team reaches twenty-two straight wins without any game being recorded as a tie. The Cleveland Indians sit alone when it comes to consecutive wins in the Majors. They broke the twenty-game win streak that was set by the Oakland Athletics back in 2002. They beat the Detroit Tigers yesterday to rewrite American League history, and they will come back tomorrow for game two and try for number twenty-three! Indians manager Terry Francona talks about win number twenty-two in the clubhouse. "You're right, they're fun games to play. The atmosphere, it kind of felt like a playoff game, and that's invaluable. We had a few opportunities, and we didn't cash in, but we kept playing. You know when you're at home, you're a hit away," Francona says.

It is a Friday night off the shores of Lake Erie, and the Cleveland Indians and the Kansas City Royals are ready to begin game two of this three-game series. Twenty-one days ago, on August 25, these two ball clubs faced one another in a three-game series when the Indians were just getting started on what has been baseball's most dominant win streak in the modern Major League era. From August 24 to September 14, the Indians have set the record for the longest win streak without any ties with twenty-two straight wins. During this streak, Cleveland has put together some of the most improbable statistics you will ever see. They have outscored their opponents by more than one hundred runs. The Indians hitters have hit more home runs than runs given up with forty-one, and the team's pitching staff has a team ERA below two. Yesterday in the series opener, the Royals had the Indians on the ropes and were one strike away from snapping the incredible twenty-one-game winning streak. The Royals' reliever, Kelvin Herrera, surrendered a two-out game tying double to Francisco Lindor in the bottom of the ninth inning that allowed the Indians to keep playing. The Indians' Jay Bruce hit the game winning single in the bottom of the tenth to score José Ramírez to start this series with a 3–2 walk-off win. Now just how long can they make it last?

We move to the top of the sixth inning at Progressive Field and have a 3–3 tie, and the Royals have the go-ahead runner standing on first base with one out. Alex Gordon has just hit a single into left field, and Terry Francona will replace the starter, Trevor Bauer, with the sidewinder Joe Smith. The Royals now have two outs, and Gordon reaches second base after the strikeout on Drew Butera and the single hit by Whit Merrifield moves up the runner. Lorenzo Cain, the center fielder, bats next, and he has reached base with hits in his last two at-bats with a single and a double. It is an even count, here comes Smith's 2–2 pitch. Cain swings and lines a single past the diving infield into center field for an RBI single. Alex Gordon comes home to give Kansas City a 4–3 advantage in the middle innings, and that will end the day for Trevor Bauer. He goes five and one-third innings and allows four runs with six strikeouts. It is the bottom half of the ninth inning in Cleveland, and the Kansas City Royals have a slim 4–3 lead and are one out away from ending this historical streak by the Indians. What better man to have up at the plate than yesterday's ninth inning hero, Francisco Lindor. The Indians are searching for that final spark to continue this game, and Lindor represents the game-winning run while Abraham Almonte is standing at first base. The Royals reliever, Mike Minor, is usually not a closer, but he has Lindor down to his final strike with a 1–2 count.

"Now the 1–2 delivery, swing and a miss the ball game's over. This historical run by the Indians comes to an end on September fifteenth. The Indians lose for the first time since August twenty-third. The Indians are coming out of the third base dugout, they're getting a standing ovation and they return the claps and applause to the Indians fans! What a moment in Downtown Cleveland!" Tom Hamilton concludes.

22 Facts about the Cleveland Indians

1. From August 24 to September 14, 2017, the Cleveland Indians set the record for the longest win streak in MLB history, winning 22 straight games. During the streak, they outscored their opponents, 142–37.

2. Before the streak began, the Indians pitching staff led the league in shutouts with 12. During the streak, they added 7 to their total, including 4 in a row at home.

3. Of the 22 games the Indians won, half of the wins came on an eleven-game road trip where they traveled to New York (Yankees), Detroit (Tigers), and Chicago (White Sox).

4. On the eleven-game road trip, the Indians played and won back-to-back doubleheaders in New York and Detroit, playing 4 games in 3 days.

5. The Tribe's second baseman, José Ramírez, had a knack for hitting home runs, particularly on the road. In total, the Indians hit 24 home runs on the road, and Ramírez was responsible for 7 of them, including 3 multihomer games.

6. Francisco Lindor, the Indians' shortstop, hit his fair share of home runs with a total of 9. His ninth home run was his thirtieth of the year—the first time ever an Indians shortstop hit 30 home runs in a single season.

7. During the streak, the Indians were not playing with a full roster. They were missing contributions from star players like Michael Brantley, Jason Kipnis, and Andrew Miller, who returned but only pitched a single inning in game 22.

8. The 22-game win streak combined for a total of 199 innings. The Indians' pitching and defense were at such a high level that Cleveland only trailed for 7.0 innings total.

9. Corey Kluber made 4 starts during the streak. He pitched 32.0 innings, struck out 35, and walked 2 batters. His final game was a complete game shutout, and at the end of the season, he was awarded his second American League Cy Young Award.

10. The Indians' Carlos Carrasco and Corey Kluber both pitched a complete game during the streak. The combined numbers of the two complete games are as follows: 18.0 IP, 17K, 0 BB, 8H, and 1ER.

11. The Indians scored first, and they scored often! The Indians took the first lead in 19 of the first 20 games of the streak.

12. August 25 to 27 was the first sweep of the win streak. Cleveland's pitching staff blanked the Kansas City Royals in a 3-game Players Weekend series. By the end of the weekend, the Indians had outscored the Royals, 20–0, with 7 home runs.

13. The Indians pitching staff from starter to reliever was on another level. By the time they had won 17 straight games, Cleveland's pitchers combined for an ERA of 1.76 over 150 innings pitched.

14. It was the second year in a row the Indians matched the franchise record for the longest win streak. In 2016, the Tribe won 14 consecutive games from June 17 to July 1, matching the previous franchise record.

15. The Universal Windows Direct company promised Indians fans free windows if the Indians broke the franchise win streak record. On Thursday, September 7, 2017, the Tribe beat their division rival, the Chicago White Sox, 11–2, and roughly $2,000,000 worth of windows were given away to Indians fans.

16. Everybody loves the long ball! During the win streak, 52 home runs were hit by the Indians and their opponents combined, and 41 came from the Tribe. That's almost 79% of them.

17. In the 22 games that the Indians won, the starting pitchers were credited with 19 wins. That's 86% of the games.

18. The Indians didn't need to worry about playing from behind too often. 21 of the 22 games ended in 9 innings.

19. On September 10, the Indians beat the Orioles to complete their fifth straight sweep. They took over first place in the American League, leading second place Houston by one game.

20. On September 12, the Indians tied the record for the longest win streak in American League history, winning 20 in a row to tie the Oakland A's of 2002. It was just the second time an American League team had won 20 straight games.

21. On September 14, 2017, The Indians won their twenty-second consecutive game in walk-off fashion. Francisco Lindor hit a two-out game-tying double in the bottom of the ninth inning. Jay Bruce hit a game-winning RBI single in the tenth inning to beat the Royals, 3–2.

22. On September 15, 2017, the Cleveland Indians were playing for their twenty-third straight win. Trevor Bauer took the loss, and after the game in the clubhouse, he said it wasn't the first time he blew a twenty-two-game winning streak. In 2010, the UCLA Bruins men's baseball team had a record of 22–0 when Trevor Bauer lost game 23 to Stanford as a sophomore pitcher.

The quotes that are used in this book come from the top three broadcasters of the Cleveland Indians and arguably in all of Major League Baseball—Matt Underwood, Jim Rosenhaus, and Tom Hamilton.

Matt Underwood started his eighteenth season in 2017 as a broadcaster for the Indians. This was his eleventh season in the TV booth calling every ball game on Fox SportsTime Ohio alongside his partner, Rick Manning.

Jim Rosenhaus started his eleventh season in 2017 as a member of the Indians radio broadcast team. Prior to 2017, he had been Tom Hamilton's partner since 2012, calling the fourth and fifth innings of every ball game on the popular MLB radio network WTAM1100.

Tom Hamilton is considered as "the voice of the Cleveland Indians." The 2017 season marked the twenty-eighth season of calling Tribe games on WTAM1100. During that time, Tom Hamilton has called eighty-four postseason games, including three world series for the Indians in 1995, 1997, and 2016. Tom works alongside Jim Rosenhaus, providing play-by-play commentary for the fans for a full 162 game season. Tom Hamilton joined the Indians radio network at the start of the 1990 season alongside his partner, Herb Score, until 1997. Tom Hamilton was born on August 19,1954 in Waterloo, Wisconsin. Tom lives with his beautiful wife, Wendy, with four children—two boys and two girls—in Avon Lake, Ohio.

Cody Allen: "Pollo"
Shawn Armstrong: "Armie"
Trevor Bauer: "Bauer Outage"
Michael Brantley: "Dr. Smooth" (On the disabled list)
Jay Bruce: "Bruuuce"
Carlos Carrasco: "Cookie"
Mike Clevinger: "Sunshine"
Edwin Encarnacion: "EE"
Yan Gomes: "Gomer"
Erik Gonzalez: "La Parita"
Nick Goody: "Goods"
Brandon Guyer: "BG"
Austin Jackson: "AJax"
Jason Kipnis: "Kip"
Corey Kluber: "Klubes"
Francisco Lindor: "Mr. Smile"
Zach McAllister: "Z-Mac"
Andrew Miller: "Miller Time" (On the disabled list)
Tyler Olson: "Oly"
Dan Otero: "OT"
Roberto Perez: "Bebo"
Jose Ramirez
Danny Salazar: "Sally" (On the disabled list)
Carlos Santana: "Slamtana"

Bryan Shaw: "Geek"
Joe Smith: "Sidewinder"
Josh Tomlin: "Scrubs"
Giovanny Urshela: "Gio"
Bradley Zimmer: "Machine"

About the Author

Author Nicholas Brigeman was born in Akron, Ohio, in 1992 and grew up in a small town near Cleveland. He is an avid supporter of all Cleveland sports teams and has taken particular interest in baseball and the Cleveland Indians since he was very young. Nicholas is currently a Tribe season ticket holder and attends as many games as possible, though he enjoys listening to Tom Hamilton call the games he cannot attend.

CPSIA information can be obtained
at www.ICGtesting.com
Printed in the USA
BVHW030209130519
548106BV00001B/115/P

9 781644 620106